# broken

## a life story

W0010476

**CFI**
**Springville, Utah**

# broken

## a life story

david john dickson
with
david briggs

© 2006 David John Dickson and David Briggs
All rights reserved.

No part of this book may be reproduced in any form whatsoever, whether by graphic, visual, electronic, film, microfilm, tape recording, or any other means, without prior written permission of the publisher, except in the case of brief passages embodied in critical reviews and articles.

ISBN 13: 978-1-55517-983-0
ISBN 10: 1-55517-983-5

Published by CFI, an imprint of
Cedar Fort, Inc., 2373 W. 700 S., Springville, UT, 84663
Distributed by Cedar Fort, Inc., www.cedarfort.com

LIBRARY OF CONGRESS CATALOGING-IN-PUBLICATION DATA

Dickson, David, 1976-
  Broken : a life story / written by David Dickson ; illustrated by Micah A. Clegg.
    p. cm.
  ISBN 1-55517-983-5
  I. Title.

PS3604.I305B76 2006
813'.6--dc22

                        2006029168

Cover design by Nicole Williams
Cover design © 2006 by Lyle Mortimer
Illustrated by Micah A. Clegg

Printed in the United States of America

10   9   8   7   6   5   4   3   2   1

Printed on acid-free paper

# Dedication

To Alice, whoever you are.

—David John Dickson

Dedicated in loving memory of my brother Bill
for his strength and support throughout the years.

—David Briggs

# Introduction

This book consists of two parts: fiction and nonfiction. It is important when reading to realize which is which. The character you will come to know as Alice is fiction. She does not exist. The events that happen to her do not reflect any specific person of whom I am aware.

The life story that David Briggs tells her, however, is true.* Everything he shares with her actually happened. Alice's existence in this book serves merely as a tool to fully convey the poignant experiences of a man who possesses more courage than I can imagine.

---

*Some of the names have been changed to protect identity.

What's gone and what's past help should be past grief.

—William Shakespeare

# Chapter 1

The building looked like a stiff breeze would topple it over. Three stories high, the structure might as well have been a house of cards built atop a slanted table. Grime-covered bricks crumbled on the building exterior. The foundation had long since been compromised, making the entire building slant downhill. The place seemingly wanted to die, but mankind would not let it.

Deep snowpack bowed in the flat roof somewhat, which made for lethal-sized icicles directly above the front door, the lowest part of the roof. If any one of those icicles fell the thirty feet to the front porch, they could kill.

A gust of late-winter wind cut into David as he stared at the entrance to the building, the Braxton halfway house. The dilapidated structure would have been condemned years ago if there had been anywhere else to send the residents.

The aging of the building itself didn't necessarily bother him. He remembered the Braxton house many years ago, then in much better repair; it had still been almost as bleak. The true darkness about the place lay in the fact that those sent here were truly sent to die. The city considered these residents write-offs. The bottom of the heap. People so wrapped up in grief and addictions that they were deemed lost causes. Sticking them all in one place had become the cure-all solution. If somebody couldn't sober up or reform in other institutions, the final step was to let them rot here.

*Who could possibly hope to get well in such an environment?* David wondered. Prisons fostered more hope.

David took a deep breath of clean air and ascended the steps to the front door, warily keeping an eye on the icicles above as he walked across the porch and entered the building.

Shadows engulfed him instantly in the dimly lit, nearly windowless front room. Squinting against the dark interior, David gagged on the pungent stench of urine and bile that always saturated the air in this place.

"Excuse me," David said, trying to catch the attention of the attendant.

The man looked up from the television, brushed aside his unkempt hair, and fixed David with a blank stare. The man absentmindedly nursed a bottle of beer.

David winced. Alcohol in a halfway house. How helpful.

"I'm here to see Alice Chambers."

The man took a long swig of his drink before answering. "Room 212."

Considering the matter over, he turned back to whatever show he had been watching.

Not for the first time, David wondered why this place even bothered with the pretense of an attendant. They did nothing. Any drug dealer or would-be thief could enter these walls unchallenged. Nobody could be expected to overcome their demons under such conditions.

But nobody who checked in here, David reminded himself, was expected to get better. Like a leper colony, the residents were left to their own vices until the vices killed them. He hated this place for that reason alone. He hated what it represented.

David decided to take the stairs. The elevator, which might as well have been an outhouse, he avoided at all costs. While climbing to the second story, he saw a man passed out in the corner. He kept moving. He had seen enough of that type in here and wondered briefly if Alice would be another of them.

David glanced back once more at the man in a heap on the ground. Unfortunately, the expectations with regard to the residents in here turned out to be right more often than not. Suicides were rampant. And the residents usually held no better expectations for themselves than did society. Most who ended up here eagerly waited for death to take them.

In all the times that David had visited the Braxton house over the years, he had only met four or five people that would even talk with him. Of those, only one had recovered. Dismal odds, though remembering the one young man who eventually straightened out his life gave David the courage to continue visiting here.

He knocked softly on the door, not sure what to expect. He only knew the twenty-three-year-old woman had checked in two days earlier. An estranged aunt of Alice's had asked him to come. She told him she hadn't spoken to Alice in years, that they had never really known each other well, yet she believed Alice was a good person. He had promised the aunt that he would visit Alice.

"Come in," a voice answered flatly.

David opened the door and took in the room. Gray paint peeled from the cinder block walls. The only pieces of furniture consisted of a bed, a single end table, and two wooden chairs. A small refrigerator sat in one corner, too rust-covered to detect the original paint color. On the end table, a television played a daytime talk show that the young woman didn't seem to be watching. Instead, she sat on the edge of the bed and stared out the window, her back to him. She never bothered to turn around.

Filtered sunlight shone dully through years of grime on the cracked glass. It did little to brighten the room. No decorations or pictures hung on the walls.

It looked like the waiting room for one about to enter purgatory.

Alice finally glanced up when David flicked off the television. She fixed a questioning glare on him, demanding him with her eyes to spit out why he'd come. Dark auburn hair hung in strands and tangles, crowning her thin and pale body. She might have been pretty once, but sorrow etched deeply into her features now, hardening them. Though young enough to be his daughter, she appeared much older.

"My name is David Briggs. Would you mind if I sat down?"

"Do I know you?" she answered, turning to gaze back through the window.

*Here goes,* David thought. "No, not yet. I know your Aunt Amelia, however. She asked me to check on you."

Even from his vantage point, David could see Alice roll her eyes.

"Aunt Amelia. You must be a church man."

"I am her bishop, yes."

A few moments passed. At last she turned back to look him in the eye.

"Tell her I'm doing just fine and the food's great." She smiled briefly, a grossly inadequate attempt to play the part of contented resident.

"Beyond that, I'm sorry. I have no interest in speaking to you or hearing about your church. But thanks for coming. Give my regards to my aunt." Alice turned to the window yet again, considering the conversation over.

David hesitated. For the brief moment she had faced him, he saw a degree of pain and torment he hadn't witnessed in years. It nearly took his breath away. Most of the people sent here were so far gone they were numb to the weight of the world. Alice, however, was still being crushed by it. Tormented by it. Her palpable suffering took him quite by surprise.

Memories of his own past seeped to the surface as David glanced about the room in brooding silence. How well he understood the emotions engraved on her face. He cleared his throat while thinking of what to say next. A tiny voice in the back of his mind whispered that this would be anything but a simple visit.

He noticed a single framed photograph on the end table, that of a little girl age three or four smiling and eating an ice cream cone.

"Who is the picture of?" David asked quietly.

"I asked you to leave," answered Alice, her voice catching.

Insight flooded into David as he regarded the picture. This woman's pain was connected to, perhaps even caused entirely by, the beautiful child in the photograph. He knew it instantly.

David gestured to the picture. "That's your daughter, isn't it?"

Alice nodded.

"Where is she now?" David asked, though he could already guess the answer.

"Morgan cemetery," Alice responded, her voice trained again back again into complete monotone.

"Do you want to talk about it?"

"No."

Silence filled the room for a span.

"It gets better you know," David said. "The pain."

Alice closed her eyes in agitation and sighed heavily.

"David, you seem like a nice enough man, so let me spare us both a lot of wasted effort." She stood and looked him dead in the eye. "You can't fix me. You can't save my soul, and you won't 'win me over for Jesus.' I'm not the candidate for your little mercy mission that you thought I might be."

She leaned in close. "Will that relieve you of whatever warped sense of responsibility that brought you here in the first place? Now I'm asking you again, please leave. Go home and wash your hands of me, or whatever you people do."

Cold menace stole over her face momentarily as she leaned in even further.

"And don't speak to me about my daughter."

David took a moment to compose himself. The biting sarcasm didn't phase him. Her penetrating eyes, though, did much more than that. For the briefest moment those eyes had betrayed the true depths of her torment within. They were windows to a soul so completely awash in anguish that he knew there could be little room in her for anything else. He was surprised she wasn't dead.

Seeing such naked grief triggered emotions and memories within David he had thought long buried and dealt with. Without consciously thinking to do so, he spoke words he would never have guessed might come up in this visit.

"When I was three years old, my mother went to work in a bar."

Alice shot him a look of complete exasperation. "Excuse me?"

"A bar," David continued. "She was gone all the time. So often, in fact, that she would often place blankets over the windows during the day so us kids would think it was night and would sleep. We hardly ever saw her."

"Why are you telling me this?"

"I don't know yet," David answered truthfully.

Three-year-old David woke up and peeked across the room. His mother was home at last, and laying on the couch.

"Mommy," he whispered. "Are you awake?"

When she didn't answer, he tiptoed to her side and stared into her face. She was sleeping. Mommy always looked like an angel when she slept. David stared at her for a few minutes, smiling.

Careful not to wake her, David snuggled up behind his mother and pressed next to her. It felt so good to be near her again. She was so warm and her hair felt so soft. David hugged her while he lay there, breathing in her perfume.

David knew that angels couldn't always be around but he wished so badly that they could. He imagined what it would be like to have her there all the time. It could never come true, he knew, except he still liked to think about it sometimes. Oh, it would be the best thing in the whole wide world. He'd never be sad again. He knew he wouldn't.

For now, he just enjoyed having her there as long as he could, and tried to stay quiet. If she didn't wake up, then she couldn't leave. David closed his eyes and snuggled some more, hoping she would sleep for a long, long time.

"David, that's a sad story, and I don't mean to seem rude, but forgive me if I'd rather not hear about your unhappy childhood. Do you want me to feel sorry for you? Okay, I do. It would be nice if we all had moms who were around all the time." She flicked a strand of hair away from her face. "I have no clue what you're hoping to accomplish by telling me this."

Alice wrapped her arms around her slender frame and regarded David with a mixture of curiosity and confusion. She had sat back down on the edge of her bed.

David took a deep breath. "I think you need to understand how broken I was. To know that you're not alone."

"Broken?" She laughed a little sarcastically. "Over that? David, my parents weren't all that great either. If they weren't screaming at me, they were screaming at each other. That's tough, all right, maybe even tragic, but it didn't break me. Not even close. You have no idea what real pain is."

Her eyes strayed instinctively to the photo of her daughter as she wrapped her arms tightly around herself once more. Before answering, David took a moment to formulate his thoughts. This was not going to be easy.

"Alice, I'd be blind if I didn't see how much pain you're in right now. It cuts me deep just to see it."

She laughed sarcastically. "Well I suggest you leave, then. Wouldn't want you to suffer because of me."

"Please. I have no intention of trying to prove anything, or make light of your own sorrow. But let me say a couple things first, and then I'll leave if you still want me to. There are some things I think you need to know."

Alice shrugged.

"First, I want you to know that I feel a strong need to share with you some pretty personal things from my life. Things I've told maybe a handful of people." He took a deep breath. "Why, I don't really know yet, except there are no strings attached. This has nothing to do with your aunt."

Now he had her attention, if not yet her interest.

David gestured again to the picture on the nightstand.

"Second, just as I can have no idea how painful the loss of your daughter is to you, you likewise can't yet know anything about me."

For the first time, she addressed him with something other than disdain. "You're right. I'm sorry. That wasn't fair of me."

She seemed sincere.

David sighed inwardly in relief. A small step forward at last.

"No apology needed," he said softly. "Alice, why are you in here?"

"Officially, alcohol, though I don't bother with it anymore. After a couple of years I realized it wasn't helping."

"I'm impressed," David said. "It took me many years before I came to that conclusion about drinking."

Alice arched an eyebrow.

"Alcohol buries pain," David explained. "I imagine that's why you started as well."

She nodded.

David clasped his hands together, deep in thought. He took a deep breath. "Alice, if you're willing to hear me out, I can say up front that it won't be easy for me to talk about some of what I will tell you. I'm willing to open this Pandora's box on my past, though, not because I want to, but because I feel I must."

He locked eyes with her once more. "I think I have something to say that you very much need to hear. Something that may in fact help you."

For a few moments she remained unreadable until a small trace of desperate hope finally cracked the cool exterior of her face. David knew he had finally reached her at least in some small, barely perceptible way. Alice folded her hands on her lap and nodded toward the chair.

"I'm listening," was all she said.

None knows the weight of another's burden.

—George Herbert

# Chapter 2

"The neighbors would occasionally find me all alone outside the post office, wearing only diapers," David said. "Sometimes even in the middle of winter. I don't remember a lot of that, really, except that it seemed like Mom and Dad always left us alone. My older sister Linda, Mom's daughter from her first marriage, took care of us as best she could. She was only three years older than Billy, though."

Alice listened in silence.

"Dad tried to make things work in our family for awhile, but he could only do so much. Mostly because of how frequently he was gone. He'd take off for weeks or months at a time working. Between that and drinking, we didn't see him very often at all."

"That must have been hard," Alice said, her voice emotionless.

"Yes," David replied. "One of the most damaging things that can ever happen to a person is to be deprived of that nurturing as a child. It was more destructive to me than anything that followed."

David could tell that Alice only listened to him out of some strained effort to act polite. He knew that her patience wouldn't last much longer if he couldn't start making sense quickly.

Though he sensed the time for chitchat had passed, he had difficulty knowing where to begin. He certainly hadn't intended on bringing any of this up when he had agreed to come visit Alice.

He knew that ultimately he'd crack open the vault and bring out everything he had to, though starting the ball rolling seemed a little daunting. He had so much to tell.

He could only begin at one logical place, David decided. When everything started to fall apart. She had to know this story in its entirety. From the beginning.

"Things really took a turn for the worse when they finally decided to get a divorce. I was five years old at the time."

"Divorces are sad," Alice offered flatly.

David nodded.

"This one, for sure. When Mom left him for another man, it took the fire right out of him. Dad had a lot of women in his life, yet he never really loved any of them except for Mom.

"As for us kids, we were lost and confused about life in a way I have a hard time describing. And as for me personally, on the day of the divorce I did something I would regret for many, many years to come."

He knew that he had her attention once more, and he hoped only that he could make the words come out right. Too much lay at stake here, he knew, for a trivial slip.

With a deep breath, he continued.

David scooped up a handful of rocks while walking to the canal in front of his house. He loved coming home again from his uncle's place, though he wished that meant the family was getting back together. Not the other way around. He plopped down by the water.

The uncovered canals in his farming community almost overflowed today. The water moved pretty fast in the summer. If he could have forgotten for even a couple of hours about meeting the judge, he'd probably have wanted to race stick boats. It was a perfect day for it. But meeting the judge terrified him too much to think about anything else.

He took off his shoes, rolled up his pants, and stuck his feet into the cold water. One at a time, he slowly tossed the pebbles into the canal.

Frustrated, David began throwing the rocks harder, making bigger splashes. The past few months didn't make any sense. Mom had moved out for good. Dad, even when he was home, always seemed sad. He had never seen Dad like this before.

David wondered if he had upset Mom or Dad by being naughty somehow. Or if Mom moved out because he and Billy wrestled too much, or woke her up sometimes when she slept. He just didn't know. The past few months he had tried so hard to do better, except it hadn't helped.

Then he and Billy had to go live with different uncles. David didn't like living with his uncle. He treated him nice enough, but it didn't compare to living with Mom and Dad.

David realized then that his own house was smaller than his uncle's. It only had one long main room and a bedroom off to the side. He worried whether or not judges cared about things like big or small houses. Sometimes it could seem pretty crowded in there with five kids and Mom and Dad. He didn't mind that, though. It was home.

He feared that after today he would have to go to his uncle's house again. Lots of things scared him about what would happen after today. David threw another rock into the canal.

The front door opened, and Billy came out to sit next to David. Billy looked confused. David could guess the reason. Dad told them earlier to think about who they wanted to live with, in case the judge asked.

"Hey," Billy said.

"Hey."

For a while they sat in silence, throwing rocks into the water.

"So who are you gonna tell the judge you wanna' live with?" David asked.

Billy shrugged. "I hope he doesn't ask us."

"What if he does?"

"I dunno. That I want to live here, I guess."

David nodded. "Me too. How's KrisAnn?"

"Still crying."

His baby sister cried a lot. Especially lately. The doctor said it would go away after a year or two and until then they had to use some medicines to keep her feeling better when she got like this. Most of the time they didn't have the medicines around, though.

Their dad had given them some spending money a little while back and David spent his to buy the medicine for her, but they'd already used it up. He wished they had saved some for today. Her crying might make the judge mad.

"You scared?" Billy asked.

David closed his eyes a moment. "Yeah," he answered. And not only a little scared, either. *Really* scared. "How about you?"

Billy nodded.

As he sat there, David realized how little he knew about judges. For one thing, he didn't know if they yelled and screamed or if they were nice. He didn't know what kind of questions they would ask, or if they pounded that hammer on the desk if somebody didn't answer them fast enough. Mostly, he didn't want to go to the courthouse at all. *Why couldn't Mom and Dad fix things so they wouldn't have to go?*

No matter how many different ways he thought about what might happen today, none of them sounded any good. He didn't want his mom to move out, and he didn't want to live with his uncle. He didn't want Billy or his sisters to live with other relatives. But it didn't seem like he could do anything about it.

"Let's grab something to eat," David suggested. All this thinking had made him pretty frustrated. The two of them walked back silently to the house, even though neither of them were actually hungry. He wished Linda hadn't gone to stay with Mom already. He missed her. She always took care of them. If she were around, he'd have lots of questions to ask her.

His two little sisters waited in the backyard. Catherine was one year younger than David, and KrisAnn wasn't even two years old yet. None of them seemed old enough to make a decision like the one Dad said the judge might ask them.

Catherine liked to sit under the big oak tree when she had lots to think about. He saw her holding KrisAnn under the tree, rocking her, trying to quiet her. Dad still hadn't come out from the bedroom.

He wondered again if judges sent kids to live with their uncles if they had to sleep on the kitchen floor at their real house. He hoped not. It really was a small home, David knew, yet he didn't mind sleeping in the kitchen. Neither did Billy. They could do it some more. Maybe he could lie to the judge and say he had his own bedroom with a real bed.

Trying to figure out what to tell the judge about bedrooms, David opened the refrigerator and pulled out a few pieces of bologna. Billy grabbed an apple and a handful of stale crackers. They ate in silence while waiting for Dad. Almost time to go.

A few minutes later, Dad came out of the bedroom, dressed to leave. His red eyes told David that he'd been crying, something he had never seen him do. Dad was the toughest guy in town. Nobody messed with him. It scared David to see Dad like this.

"Let's go," Dad said to David and Billy. Then he went outside and grabbed Catherine and KrisAnn.

They all piled into the car without a word. Dad started the engine and pulled out of the driveway. He turned the car toward town and hit the gas.

David's stomach tightened. They were really going. He couldn't stop it. Everything still played out like a bad dream and the moving car made the nightmare all the more real.

As the car continued rolling through his neighborhood, he kept thinking that in a couple hours things would get messed up forever if somebody didn't stop it. They were running out of time.

The rolling hills and green fields passed by too fast. He wished Dad would drive slower. He needed time to think.

Catherine smoothed the folds of her flower-print dress. Her blonde hair sparkled in the morning sunlight, making her look more like an angel than a four-year-old trying to figure out where to spend the rest of her life.

After a few minutes of driving, Catherine finally broke the silence. "Daddy, I wants to live with Mommy and you." She cleared her throat. "Both at the same time. Please? I'll be really good."

David agreed completely. He could be better too. He could work harder. He didn't mind doing the dishes. Or cleaning the house. Or weeding the yard. Anything.

Billy nodded in agreement.

When Dad didn't answer Catherine right away, David's heart leapt. They still had a chance!

"Yeah, Dad," David said. "Billy and I can work harder too. Lots and lots harder. We'll help out with KrisAnn more if you need us to. And do our chores super fast." David would do anything if he thought it might make a difference.

Dad finally turned back to David, sadness on his face. "I know you would, Half Pint." David smiled at hearing Dad's nickname for him. He hadn't used it much lately. Dad cleared his throat.

"Kids, you're doing great. You haven't done anything wrong. This is between me and your mom. I'm sorry." His voice sounded very far away. "Just be thinkin' about what you want to do if the judge asks you."

Several long minutes later, Dad pulled into the parking lot at the courthouse. The two-story building looked big and scary. They walked inside the front door where an older man in a uniform told them to go into the main courtroom. The judge would come in soon.

The courtroom had lots of benches and a great big, high desk at the front. Hardly anybody was in the courtroom. Even empty, it scared David. The pictures on the walls of people David didn't recognize all seemed to glare at him as if he'd done something wrong. Flags hung from the ceiling. Everything looked clean and organized. He didn't like walking into such an important room.

Dad made them sit on the front bench while he walked back and forth. David didn't see his mother or his older sister Linda. *They must be running a little late,* he guessed. The high bench kept David's feet well off the ground. He suddenly felt very, very small. Glancing at his brother and sisters, he could at least tell that they didn't like this any more than he did. KrisAnn, sitting on Catherine's lap, started to cry.

David stared around the empty courtroom and swallowed the fear rising inside of him. Families broke apart in this room, he realized. Here, moms and dads and brothers and sisters all went different ways.

Suddenly, a lady announced the judge. Everybody stood up as the judge walked into the room. David stood as well, though he didn't understand why he needed to. He thought people stood up for kings and queens, but he didn't realize that they did that for judges. Judges were even more important than he had guessed. The realization made him even more nervous than before.

The judge told them all to sit down and then asked the four kids to come into his chambers. David and his siblings slid off the bench and followed.

The judge left the room and an assistant led the four of them toward the same doorway. As they followed the older woman and before they left the courtroom, Mom walked in through the back door. Linda wasn't with her. KrisAnn saw Mom right away and started screaming for her. David tried to silence his baby sister as they followed the judge's assistant out of the room and down a long hallway.

The assistant opened a door and led them into a quiet room with a big desk and a few stuffed chairs. The judge sat at the desk, reading something. None of the kids wanted to sit down, and KrisAnn still cried hysterically for her mommy. The assistant came in the room behind them and closed the door.

Without speaking to them yet, the judge opened a black notebook and began to write in it. Billy, David, and Catherine sat in silence while KrisAnn wailed. As David stood there waiting for the judge to say something, he grew more and more nervous. When KrisAnn simply wouldn't calm down for Catherine, David asked if he should try and quiet her. Sometimes he could make her smile.

Catherine nodded and gave him their baby sister. He tried the silly faces, the tummy tickles, pats on the back—everything. She only cried louder.

Normally her crying didn't bother him so much. He had grown used to it by now. But today it felt like KrisAnn screamed out loud what they all knew deep inside. That no matter what Mom and Dad said about things being okay, this was terrible. The worst thing that could ever happen.

The judge stopped writing at last and turned toward them. David's stomach dropped. The judge looked awfully mean. He seemed to frown even when he smiled.

"You don't have to be afraid," the judge said. He took off his glasses and rubbed his eyes. He tried smiling down at them, although David knew better than to feel happy. He had nothing to smile about. In only a few minutes this man would split his family apart.

"Okay, kids," the judge said as he glanced down at them, "you know your Mommy and Daddy aren't going to live together any more, right?"

Nobody spoke. David finally answered for all of them. "Yes, we know that."

The judge nodded.

"And that means your family won't all be in the same house any more, right?"

Still, nobody spoke. KrisAnn kept on wailing away and David patted her back some more. Sometimes that helped a little. But he didn't think she cried this time because of stomach pains. She cried about something a lot worse.

"Right?" the judge repeated.

"Right," David answered.

The judge rubbed his eyes again as if he had a headache.

"So, I'd like you to tell me who you want to live with."

David turned to Billy for support, but his brother only stared at the ground. Catherine didn't say anything either.

"Um, we want to live with our dad," David finally answered. At least he thought they all did. He wondered why Catherine and Billy weren't talking.

The judge put his glasses back on and leaned forward.

"All of you want to live with your dad?"

When KrisAnn kicked and twisted to be put down, David had a thought. "Well, maybe our baby sister needs Mom right now. She cries a lot for her. Sometimes only Mom can make her happy."

"I see," the judge said. "Thank you for telling me that." He scribbled something down in his notebook.

David suddenly became very uncomfortable telling the judge all of this. These decisions were way too big for him to explain how they should turn out.

"At . . . at least that's what I think," David said, elbowing Billy. He glared at Catherine to speak up too. Nothing.

"Okay David, thank you for your input." The judge looked down at his brother and sister. "Catherine? Billy? Do you have anything else to add?"

David knew they probably did, yet they shook their heads.

"So you agree with your brother, then?"

They both nodded slowly, seemingly afraid to do anything more. David couldn't believe that neither Billy or Catherine had said anything. As the judge took down some more notes, David realized that he had never once asked Catherine where she wanted to live.

He also realized that even though KrisAnn cried for Mom right now, maybe she'd be better off with Dad anyway. After all, David could sometimes make her happy. And she'd have her brothers and sister around. Besides, Dad loved her too. He really did.

David nearly spoke up to give a few more thoughts on the matter when the judge cleared his throat and stood.

"Okay. That's all I need, then."

As the judge's assistant led them back into the courtroom, David started feeling worse and worse about what had just happened. He remembered all the times he had woken up without Mom in the house. Neighbors told him that they'd found him wandering around the neighborhood in diapers. He always had Linda and Billy to watch out for him, at least.

True, Linda would live with Mom and so could help with KrisAnn but what about when Linda went to school? She couldn't always be around to help. What if KrisAnn woke up with nobody home? Nobody at all?

Then she would cry and cry and cry, and no one would come. Nobody would give her tummy tickles or pat her back. Nobody would sing to her, play with her, change her diaper, or feed her a bottle!

The judge began asking his mom and dad questions, though David couldn't pay attention to them. As the meeting dragged on, he could think about nothing but his baby sister.

He saw in his imagination KrisAnn waking up alone in her new house. He could hardly stand the thought and started crying as he imagined his baby sister screaming in an empty room without anybody to hold her. Screaming so hard that her face turned red, like it did sometimes, except this time nobody would even pick her up.

David's heart pounded in panic. He thought he might throw up. He loved his sister. He couldn't bear to think about something so awful happening to her, and if it did, it would all be his fault.

For a few minutes he tried to tell himself that would never happen. His mom was marrying another man. At least one of them would always stay home to take care of her while his older sister went to school. David wanted to believe that they would. He had to believe it, because if it wasn't true and they sometimes would leave KrisAnn totally alone, then he had done something really, really bad. Because there was always the chance they *could* leave her alone, he realized.

In fact, a pretty good chance.

Tears ran down his cheeks. He had been left alone more times than he could remember. Even as a baby, like his neighbors told him. Why should she be any different? He imagined again his baby sister, thrashing on the floor, tears running down her cheeks. All by herself.

David wanted to jump up and scream that he had made a mistake.

The judge pounded his gavel and announced that he had made a decision on the custody of the children. Dad had taught them earlier that custody meant who lived with who. David held his breath.

"It is my ruling that Billy, David, and Catherine will live with the father," the judge said. "KrisAnn will live with the mother."

David's breath caught in his throat. He could hardly believe his ears. The judge did exactly what he had suggested.

Mom came over and picked up KrisAnn, smiling down at her. Linda had never come, David realized sadly. He wanted to tell her that he'd made a mistake, and maybe Linda could fix it. Linda would know what to do. But she hadn't come.

Mom said her good-byes to Catherine, Billy, and David, and promised something about seeing them all the time. That this wasn't as bad as they thought. That everything would turn out okay. The same things she had said over and over the past few months. They didn't make David feel any better. Catherine and Billy still didn't say much of anything.

At least KrisAnn had stopped crying a bit once she was in her mother's arms.

As Mom left the room with KrisAnn, however, his baby sister began screaming at full volume once again. As KrisAnn's cries sounded further and further away, David had the horrible feeling he had just made the biggest mistake of his life.

Appearances often are deceiving.

—Aesop

# Chapter 3

Alice looked disbelievingly at David. "You're kidding me. The judge let you decide the fate of your family when you were only five years old?"

"That's what it seemed like at the time. Even if the judge would have awarded it that way anyway, I always believed he did it because of what I said."

"So what happened to KrisAnn?"

"Well, a short time later, when Catherine couldn't handle being away from our little sister, she went and lived with Mom." David took a deep breath. "From that moment on, though, I felt it was my fault that the family split apart. That because of what I said to the judge, Billy and I didn't get to grow up with our sisters."

For a few silent moments, Alice absorbed those thoughts.

"That's a horrible responsibility to give such a young child," she said.

"I agree."

Sensing that Alice was ready to open up a little, David waited quietly.

"My parents were always yelling at each other," she said at length. "I honestly can't remember a single day when they didn't scream back and forth at least once."

David knew well those thoughts.

"That wasn't the worst, though. You almost get used to it after a while." Alice rubbed her hands briskly together, as if to ward off the chill of a bad memory. "The worst was them using me as a tool for leverage against each other. Time and again they tried to pit me against the other parent. You know, to convince me how the other was always wrong."

Alice closed her eyes and shook her head. "I was a game piece between them. Even on birthdays. The only birthday parties I ever got happened when one of them thought the other had forgotten. Then the one who remembered would throw me an impromptu party to make themselves look better."

"That sounds miserable," David said.

Alice nodded. "In some ways, David, I think that if my parents had divorced like yours did, I would have been much better off. At least I wouldn't have been fought over like some prize." She looked blankly out the window. "So did things improve, afterward? When you moved in with your dad?"

"I didn't move in with my dad. I moved in with my uncle. Dad still stayed away too much of the time. And Billy lived with another uncle."

"Oh. So was that better or worse than before?"

David shrugged. "Hard to say. I felt lonelier than ever for awhile, and then my dad met another woman and fell in love. Her name was Margaret, but everybody called her Ina. When Dad and Ina got engaged, Billy and I became pretty excited. Not only would we get to move back home with Dad, we would have a mom again. A mom who would actually be around the house."

"What was she like?"

*Now there's a question,* David thought. "Well, we met her a few times before the wedding and found her as kind and loving as we could want. We couldn't wait for her and Dad to marry. And she had a son, Karl, who was four years older than Billy. An older brother to look out for us too. I couldn't believe our luck. I was still only five at the time and already we had a new family."

A sad smile crept on Alice's face. "Better late than never, right?"

He could literally see Alice's defenses forging tight once more. She was making the seriously grave mistake in thinking he had already described the rough part of his life and was now giving the happy ending. Oh, that his story were so simple.

She stood and stretched her muscles. "David, I think I get your message now. Love conquers all. There's always a light at the end of the tunnel, and all that stuff. Thank you for your time, I'll give it some thought." Alice deliberately looked toward the door.

This woman radiated such pain that David wanted to weep for her. She had nothing whatsoever in her life to look forward to or work toward. He himself had been that way too many times to count and knew well how devastating life became in those circumstances. He could certainly empathize with Alice. Even so, he still wasn't reaching her. He could see the frigidity of her demeanor come and go in the space of mere breaths. He had no choice but to crack open the vault.

"If you don't mind, I have a bit more to share on the matter. Would you like to hear how Ina fit into our little family?"

Alice shrugged. "Sure. Why not?"

David knew from experience that no matter what she expected him to say, she would be wrong.

The sound of footsteps brought David awake. He hoped they belonged to Ina. After all, she hadn't given him a good night kiss. When Dad told him they were going to have a new mom, David couldn't wait for good night kisses again. It had been so long. This was already the third night after Ina and Dad had been married, and she'd forgotten each time including tonight. David's heart skipped a beat when Ina flipped on a light and he could see her clearly.

When he glanced at her face, however, David panicked. He hoped he hadn't done anything wrong. She looked really, really mad.

"Get up," she said. "Both of you."

Somehow David knew instantly that this had nothing to do with a good night kiss. He kicked Billy a couple of times who, when he woke up, seemed mad enough to kick David right back until he too noticed Ina and the frown on her face. She had never once looked that way. Ever. Holding one hand behind her back, Ina walked a few steps closer.

"Stand over there," she ordered them, pointing toward the fireplace. David and Billy were dressed only in their underwear, but did as they were told. David wondered if maybe this was some sort of game. Any moment he thought she might break out laughing and then he'd feel silly for getting fooled so easily.

Ina brought the hand out from behind her back. In it she clutched one of Dad's thick leather belts. Without warning she whipped it across David's bare chest.

Pain and confusion washed over him as he cried out involuntarily at the sting. She whipped Billy once with the belt too.

"Hey, what'd we do?!" David asked. *So much for this being a game . . .*

Ina leaned in with a sneer. "Not a word." She sat down on the sofa. "Now I want you to keep your eyes open, as punishment. Just stand there and keep them open. All night long. If you close 'em, I'm gonna whip ya."

David stared at her in shock. She wasn't kidding. He and Billy had obviously done something terrible, though he couldn't remember what. And now his new mom stood in front of them so angry that she needed to whip them over it. He felt horrible. They had disappointed Ina! He only wished he knew how.

While standing there, David became more and more mad at himself for making her angry so soon. He and Billy hadn't even lasted a week before upsetting her. No wonder she hadn't given them any good night kisses. That would all change, though. She was their new mom, and Dad had promised they would be a happy family now. David knew they would. Dad said so. He and Billy would fix whatever made her mad, once they found out what they did, and then she'd be a lot happier. Happier, like she used to be.

All through the long night, David tried and tried to think back on what he might've done wrong. He also tried, sometimes unsuccessfully, to keep his eyes open like she wanted. Each time he or Billy closed them, the belt whipped across their skin, reminding them how disappointed they'd made their new mother. He figured he must've deserved it, but still wished he could remember why!

As his eyes slid shut for a few seconds once more and she cracked the belt across his back for punishment, David made a quick promise with himself. No matter what happened in the future, he would never disappoint her like this again.

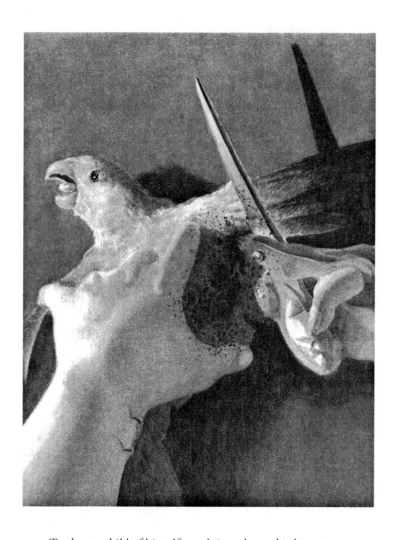

To cheat a child of his self-worth is to deny a bird its wings.

—Heather Harris

# Chapter 4

David ached everywhere. His arms and legs hurt so bad from moving the sprinkler pipe, to say nothing of the six mile walk to and from work twice a day, that he could barely move. Pulling Billy along was almost more than he could bear.

The past two years had been one big nasty surprise after another, ever since Dad and Ina got married. Worst of all, the long work days were the easy part.

He looked at Billy, riding in the wagon. His older brother was tending to a cut on his ankle, trying to clean it off as best he could. *At least we found the old wagon alongside the road,* David thought. God did watch out for them now and again—sometimes. Like today, for example. He could never have carried his brother home after everything else they'd done.

"Is your ankle still bleeding?" David asked.

"A little, but I think it'll be okay."

David walked in silence a bit longer. "Billy, do you think things will ever get better?"

Billy didn't have to ask what he meant. Getting up at 3:30 every morning, walking six miles to work, moving the heavy sprinkler pipe in the fields, walking back home and then to school—because nine times out of ten they missed the bus—and then walking back to work all over again. Afterward, they had nothing to look forward to but coming straight home to do more slavish work for Ina while Karl watched television.

"I don't know," Billy answered eventually. "At least we got paid today. That should help a little."

David hoped it would too, but he knew better than to get his hopes up. *If only Dad stayed home more often,* he wished. She was so much better then.

The sun had almost set by the time they arrived at home. As carefully as he could, David helped his brother out of the wagon and up to the house.

Anxiety began to build within David as they walked toward the door. His stomach twisted and turned as he imagined what Ina might say and do. They normally came home at least an hour before this. She would be furious, no doubt.

Opening the door slowly, David tried not to make a sound as they entered.

But Ina leapt out of the chair the moment the front door swung in. Her eyes had a crazy look that David knew so well. He braced himself for what would come next.

"So, I see you decided to come home from playing around?" She glanced outside and noticed the newly found wagon. Her face darkened. "You been out looking for toys, then?"

Billy looked down at the floor. David knew he would have to answer for the both of them.

"Billy cut his foot real bad. We had to find a way to get him home."

Ina lunged forward and backhanded Billy across the face. "Is that true?"

Billy opened his mouth, but no sound came out. He could only stare down at the floor, shaking in front of Ina. She slapped him again. Harder.

"Is it? You worthless boy, talk to me!"

David's heart broke. "Please, Ina, it was an accident. He cut his foot looking for pop bottles." He wished she would calm down. After all, she made them look for bottles in the first place. They got five cents apiece.

Without pausing, she slapped David across the face as well.

"The Bible says that children who talk back will be cursed with sickness all the days of their life. Just you think about that next time you wanna' open that mouth of yours." Karl looked up from the couch and laughed the way he always did when Ina acted this way.

Billy finally found courage to speak. "We got paid today." He fished in his pockets and handed over the few bills that they had earned. She took the money without hesitation and smiled at Billy in a way that made David sick.

"You two little bastard children really are good for nothing, aren't you? If you wasn't so worthless and stupid, you coulda' made three times this much." She stashed the money in one of her dress pockets. "People pay you mostly outta pity, anyway. The whole town knows you're not bright enough to do a good day's work."

That last comment David wanted to argue. They weren't smart, he knew, but they could work hard. Real hard. Lots of people said so. And they always found enough bottles to get a little extra money on top of what they normally earned. Still, he knew better than to say so at a time like this.

"Do your chores," she commanded. "Any more lip outta either one of you and I'll turn Karl loose."

David watched Karl pound a closed fist into an open hand, grinning at the two of them. The sight made David shiver. Karl didn't spend all those nights at the gym just to look good for the girls he chased. He could be every bit as violent as Ina.

"What chores would you like us to do?" David asked.

Looking up from counting the money, Ina thought for a moment. "Dishes, garden, front lawn. Then the woodpile. I want it over by the east side of the yard tonight."

Even Billy flinched at that last one.

David forced himself to speak. "But . . . we just moved the woodpile yesterday. I don't think Billy can with his hurt foot."

Before Ina's face could twist in distaste, Karl jumped up from the couch. "Ma, you want me to deal with them?"

Smiling, Ina patted her son's shoulder. Her real son. The one she loved. "No. Not yet. You enjoy your show for now."

Seeing how she looked at Karl with love and patience always confused David. It seemed impossible that one person could act so different from one moment to the next. She could go from nice to scary as fast as it took to drop a piece of firewood to the floor.

"Get a willow, both of you."

David closed his eyes. After all they had been through that day, and now this. He wished he could learn to keep his mouth shut. He and Billy walked outside without complaint, fearing as always to make her angrier by complaining. That he had single-handedly caused this particular beating made David feel worse than anything else.

"She shouldn't have to whip you too. This one's my fault."

Billy shook his head. "Don't worry about it. She'd have done it anyway. Let's get it over with so we can do the chores and go to bed. I'm so tired I can hardly stand up."

While they each found a good willow branch, a nice, long, thick one with the leaves stripped off, David wondered if he could somehow spare Billy getting whipped. That's the least he could do. Billy could hardly even put any weight on his injured ankle.

After all, if it weren't for David's big mouth, they could already be doing chores.

They each found a branch, and David went in first. He handed Ina his willow, and took off his shirt while she inspected it. If the branch didn't meet her expectations, she would get one herself and whip them twice as bad. Early on they learned to only get the right kind of willow.

Satisfied, she tried it out once on David's bare back. It hurt real bad, but he didn't cry out. Not unless he had to. Karl would laugh.

The whippin' started. Ina pulled the willow high over her head and brought the branch down with all her strength. The torturous whips left welts every time they lashed against his skin, but David stifled back the cries. He wouldn't give Karl reason to laugh.

He kept count, as he always did, to try and distract his mind.

Normally she would hit around twenty or thirty times, depending on her mood. It gave him something to focus on instead of the blinding pain.

She stopped at close to thirty.

"Off with your shirt, Billy."

As Billy pulled his shirt up, David found his voice again. "Please, can you not whip him? It's my fault."

She sneered down at him. Karl looked up from the couch, ready to laugh with Ina over such a ridiculous request.

"I mean, just whip me again instead."

Billy began shaking his head no, but David had already committed himself. He didn't want his brother to hurt because of something he did.

Ina looked puzzled for a second, as though she didn't know whether to get angry or laugh out loud.

But then, her entire face transformed once again. She smiled in a very scary way.

"Billy, take off your shirt. Your brother here doesn't want you to get hurt, it seems."

While Billy did so, Ina handed the bloodied willow to David. Confused, he grasped it.

"So, I think it only right that he gives you your punishment tonight, instead of me."

On the couch, Karl hooted his approval. He turned eagerly to watch this unfold, his television program forgotten.

David stared in stunned disbelief. He had to have heard wrong or misunderstood something. She couldn't actually expect him to whip his own brother.

Billy looked simply shocked.

"What do you mean?" David asked, numb to what he feared she would say.

Ina grinned again. "I mean that you're gonna whip Billy. And since you aren't as strong as me, I'd say you have to give him about forty lashes to make up for it. Oh, and if I can see that you aren't hitting as hard as you know how," she leaned in, "it'll be forty more."

Never before had David really hated this woman. Not until that moment. This was too much. Too much.

But if he protested, she would make it worse. She always did.

Silently begging his brother to forgive him, David brought the willow down hard on Billy's back. Billy cried out.

Billy's cry cut David to the core. Whether Billy cried from pain, or from having his brother whip him, David didn't know. He knew only that he hated being the one to cause it. Tears fell down David's cheek as he swung the branch again and again, counting out loud as he went.

Ina arched an eyebrow. "Not bad. Not bad at all. I told you some good would come from moving all that pipe. You're both still worthless as a dead cat, but at least you're getting some muscle on those bones. Who said you could stop?"

Closing his eyes against the hot flood of tears, David brought the willow down on his brother's back time and again. Billy's cries made David break down in sobs. This wasn't fair.

Karl began laughing hysterically, and even Ina chuckled. Both David and Billy were sobbing like they hadn't in years. After twenty lashes, David couldn't take it any more. He had to end it as quickly as possible. In the space of ten seconds or so, he whipped out the remaining twenty lashes as hard and fast as he could. He blocked out the cries in his own mind, and tried not to see the growing, bloodied welts on Billy's back.

When he finally finished, he dropped the willow and buried his face in his hands, not wanting to look at the monster in front of him. He couldn't believe what this terrible woman had made him do to his brother.

Feeling Billy's reassuring hand on his shoulder only made him feel worse.

"Don't worry Billy," Ina soothed. "You have a chance to get even. David asked to get whipped again."

"I . . . I can't," Billy said. "Please, no."

David uncovered his eyes.

Ina lowered her voice menacingly and held out the willow.

"But you heard him, Billy. This is his fault. I'm sure you understand. Or do you want me to think of something else?"

With fear on his face, Billy grasped the willow from her. He looked to David with all the empathy and apology he could.

David knew Billy's thoughts exactly. No words were needed. David turned his back to his brother, and waited.

"Out of fairness, another forty lashes should do it. And you know what happens if you hold back."

In the background, David could hear Karl burst out in laughter as Billy brought the branch down time and again.

*Please God,* David prayed, *don't let this hurt Billy as much as she wants it to.*

The branch came down time and again. This time David didn't try keeping count of the lashes. Instead, he thought of the memory that he often held onto in times like these. The memory from long ago when he snuggled up to his real mother on the couch.

He had felt loved then. He remembered feeling safe, though only for a moment. He had wanted that feeling to last forever. The crack of the willow across his flesh reminded him that those days were long gone now. His mind drifted back and forth between that cherished memory and the constant stinging on his flesh.

At long last, it ended. Karl's laughter finally died down, and his attention returned back to snacks and television.

Ina stuffed a pinch of tobacco in her mouth. "Now if your chores ain't done by the time I'm ready for bed, I'm gonna raise sand. You get it?"

They nodded, eyes cast down.

"You do the dishes," David said to Billy. "I'll start on the woodpile."

Billy nodded without comment, and David put his shirt back on, wincing in pain. Just keep moving, he reminded himself, and then Ina would finally let them sleep—the best part of the day.

✦ ✦ ✦

Alice looked as though she had been stricken with fever. With pale face and perspiring forehead, she trembled slightly while David finished describing the time Ina made he and Billy whip each other.

David still didn't fully understand why she needed to hear these painful memories. She certainly didn't enjoy hearing them, but he trusted that the reasons would surface soon enough.

Regardless, he had said enough for one day. He knew that at least.

"I think I'll head home for the night," he said. "Is there anything you need?"

Speechless, she merely shook her head.

"Alright, then. May I come back tomorrow?"

She snapped out of the fog she was in. "Sure, David. Come by whenever you like." She laughed bitterly. "It's not like I'm going anywhere."

Placing a reassuring hand on her shoulder for a moment, he turned to leave her with her thoughts and closed the door softly behind him.

Somehow or another, he had not only touched a nerve with her, he had stripped it bare. And he had barely told her the beginning. Alice had a lot to think on.

When he rounded the turn at the end of the hallway, lost in thought, David bumped into a man who instantly filled him with a sense of foreboding and warning.

He stopped and glared into the younger, muscular man's eyes. Behind the greasy hair was veiled the reptilian gaze of a predator stalking its prey. David's blood boiled at the sight.

The man sneered as David stared him down. "Hey old man, is there a problem?"

"Don't touch her."

The younger man laughed, "Whoa, don't worry Pops. I'm just gonna introduce myself. Same as you. Gets lonely around here. She could use a little company."

Had David been at the far end of the hallway, he could still not have missed the intent of naked lust in this dangerous man's eyes. David was keenly aware of the lack of guards, the absence of order, and Alice's complete state of vulnerability.

"Now step aside Pops," the man said roughly.

The young man shoved his way past David in a single motion.

Before David even hit the wall, instinct guided his hands and he lunged at the stranger in front of him. He gripped the man tightly by his broad shoulders and slammed him against the opposite wall, the anger pouring through him. He knew this type as well as he knew what this man would do to Alice if he had the chance.

"Get your hands off me!" the man screamed. "I mean now, or you're dead!"

The man drew himself up to his full height and balled his hands into fists, ready to strike, until he locked eyes with David.

David watched the man's anger turn to shock, at first, and then to naked fear. David knew what he must look like to the man right now and he made no attempt to hide it. He had caught glimpses of himself in the mirror in the past when the rage surfaced like this. His face took on the look of a caged animal let loose, one whose power was forged by a lifetime of pain.

Still pinning the man tightly to the wall with one hand, David released the other hand from his shoulder and brought it to the man's throat, squeezing hard. The man's eyes widened in fear as he felt the strength in those hands. David leaned in and spoke with a voice that would frighten a killer.

"I know why you're here. You're not welcome. Leave. Lay a hand on her, and you'll regret it for the rest of your life."

Once David finally relaxed his grip, the man staggered toward the exit. A safe distance off, he finally shouted back.

"You're insane, you old pervert! She's all yours. I hope you catch something fatal from her!" Then the man sprinted down the stairs and out the building.

It took David a few minutes to calm down and pull back from the black hole he had so nearly slid into. The very sight of a man intent on harming another human being unleashed a wave of powerful emotions so intense that they could have reduced the man to living life in a wheelchair if David had given in to them. Seeing an innocent person in harm's path still had that effect on David, even all these years later. He suspected that it always would.

At length, he unclenched his fists, took several deep breaths, and walked out the building, wondering again how anybody could ever expect to get well in a place such as this.

Only in quiet waters do things mirror themselves undistorted.
Only in a quiet mind is adequate perception of the world.

—Hans Margolius

# Chapter 5

The halfway house conveyed an even deeper sense of menace under the full cover of night. David's muscles hurt. He had planned on coming earlier in the evening, but the roof collapse during the day's job had set back his plans. The rotten timbers had given way all at once. Miraculously, he hadn't sustained any injuries from the incident. It would take a few days to clear out the debris, let alone rebuild the framing for the roof.

Even so, he was determined to visit with Alice again tonight. David wondered what she had thought about yesterday's visit. It was strange, the incidents he had brought up with her. He had shared them with so few throughout the years. Not only did it bring up memories he would rather not think about, it often upset the listener.

He entered the building, not bothering to speak with the attendant who scarcely glanced up anyway. Part of him thought to grab the scrawny man by his shirt and shake him until his bones rattled. 'Anyone could come in here!' he wanted to shout at the worthless gatekeeper.

As he knocked softly on Alice's door, he tried to decide where he could possibly begin this time. He hoped he would know when the time came. Though he had only known her for a day, she already felt like a daughter. And not just any daughter—a daughter in dire trouble. His heart ached to know how to help her.

Alice answered, bleary-eyed, looking as though she'd been crying for hours on end. David could not detect a trace of joy on her face—only a tragic and complete sadness.

This wasn't going to be easy.

"David."

The rigidity with which she spoke taught him plenty. An all-out war was being waged over this girl and he knew the winning side at the moment.

"Hello, Alice. I thought I'd check and see how you're doing again, if that's okay. Is everything all right?"

She didn't mince words. "No, David, everything is not all right. I'm in my own private hell, actually. Your words haven't exactly helped either. I'd like you to leave."

"Alice, I'm only trying to—"

"Listen, David. I'm not so heartless that I can't feel sorry for what you've been through, but your stories gave me nightmares all night."

She took a deep breath, wrapping her arms tightly around herself, as if to ward off the memories.

"You mean to help me," she continued. "I can see that. You have a good heart." She leveled him with a glare of finality. "But you're only making things worse. What you shared with me last night was the last thing I need to hear. My heart can't take any more grief than it already—"

"How old was your daughter, Alice?" The question popped out without his thinking to ask it. David sent a silent prayer of thanks heavenward as she scrunched up her face in surprise.

"What?"

"Your daughter. How old was she before she died?"

Alice waited a few moments, uncertainty playing on her face. "Lily was five. Why?"

David ignored the question. "Oh, that's a fun age. I have a five-year-old granddaughter right now. All she ever wants to do is somersault and cartwheel around the house, although one of her more exuberant cartwheels ended up almost breaking the dining room window."

Alice couldn't suppress a laugh.

The radiant smile and resulting transformation on Alice's face struck so powerful a contrast it nearly frightened David. She appeared to have come from the deepest recesses of purgatory to the brightest circle of heaven in the span of two or three seconds.

"Lily had a streak of that in her too, but her weakness was for the dramatic."

David smiled back. "You mean like puppet shows?"

Alice laughed, clean and long. "Yes! But she soon tired of simple puppet theater. After that, she started adding pretend symphonies, piano recitals, opera concerts, and then finally acting out entire movies or plays for her audience of one. Me."

"That's precious. When did she start all that?"

Alice deliberated a moment, apparently uncertain whether she wanted to go into this. At last her features relaxed and she broke into a wistful grin.

"Well, it all started a little before her third birthday. We were visiting a friend who had a piano." She looked happily lost in the memory. "I asked Lily if she wanted to hear mommy play a song."

Alice closed her eyes for a moment. "I still remember how excited she became. I had never played for her before. At that time, I hadn't touched a piano in at least four or five years. Lily's eyes widened as if I'd told her I had wings or something."

David smiled at the description. "So what did you play?"

"Oh, nothing really. A simple tune. I was pretty out of practice. But it might as well have been a concerto to Lily. She clapped until her hands hurt." She took a deep breath. "Once upon a time I actually played very well—music became my one escape while growing up. I played constantly. Besides, if I could play loud enough my parents couldn't hear to argue with each other."

David nodded. She loved music. He would remember that. "So let me guess, she made you play all the time after that?"

A smile of pure happiness spread across her face. "Oh yes. We had to go to the community center every evening. They had a piano we could use without charge. Lily wanted me to teach her, as well. She was making good progress, too, until . . . "

As her voice trailed off, the mask of happiness crumbled to dust and one of anger replaced it.

"Do you know what that feels like, David?" She spewed the words out as an accusation. Her body shook with anger, directed at everything at once. "I know you're life was rough. Worse than mine, in fact. But you've obviously found something to fill the void. I won't. Not again."

She wiped free a tear before continuing. "My whole life had amounted to one big disaster before Lily came into it. Nobody loved me. Ever. Not even the bastard who fathered her. Then Lily was born and my whole world changed. She became my lifeline. She made everything worth it."

She pointed an accusing finger skyward. "And God took her away from me when some drunk driver slumped behind the wheel and plowed his pickup right into my car."

Tears streamed freely down her face. David's heart broke at the sight.

"He never received a scratch," she said. "Not a scratch. Tell me, David, where is the justice in that? What kind of a God would let something like that happen?"

David regarded her a moment. The time had not yet come to answer that question.

"Did she suffer?" he asked quietly.

"Thankfully, no. Hey, I should feel grateful, right?" Sarcasm laced her every move. "Don't you see, David, I have nothing left. Nothing at all. When she was alive, Lily completely made up for everything I'd ever missed out on, but now she's gone. I have nothing left to live for."

"I disagree."

She laughed bitterly once more. "Oh, that's right. I have God. I have Jesus." Alice clenched her hands into white-knuckled fists. "Tell me one thing, David. One thing, only. And answer honestly. Have you ever stared death square in the face and invited it right in the door?"

Alice threw open her door in mock example, gesturing in dramatically. "Invited it in because you had no reason to chase it back? Because you had no hope whatsoever, nothing to live for, and might just as well die than live another day?"

Taking a deep breath before answering, David met her accusatory stare eye for eye.

"Yes."

Suspicion laced her features, but the longer she held his gaze the more she seemed to believe him.

Intrigue replaced suspicion, but a trace of doubt remained. "No, I mean where you literally didn't care if you died. In fact, you would've welcomed it."

"Yes."

Her defenses faded once more. The slightest vestige of hunger for help showed.

"And . . . and how did you get past that?"

"Mind if I come in first? Hey, if you'll let death inside, surely an old man is no worse?"

Finally, a laugh! It was worth it, even if he had to call himself old. Fifty wasn't even close, but she didn't know that yet.

As she gestured him inside, David prepared himself for what he would tell her next.

✦ ✦ ✦

Karl slammed a fist into David's side, knocking the wind out of him completely. David fell to the ground, gasping for air.

Ina stood over him, glaring with contempt. "You worthless boy, you have the nerve to wet your sheets? Do you think we can afford to replace them?"

She gestured to Karl to pick him up.

David winced as his step-brother hauled him up, but dared not protest. She would only get meaner if he did. He tried to hide the accident from her all day long, but she finally found out.

As Karl held him in place, Ina took a moment to shove a

cigarette in her mouth, then ground it up as chewing tobacco.

Sneering, Ina spat a glob of tobacco-laced saliva at David. A trail of dark juice dribbled down her chin. "You're worthless, you know that? You're stupid, lazy, and don't mind nobody. I told ya not to wet your sheets again. Didn't I tell ya?"

Yes, she had. He usually went to bed thirsty every night, but it was so hard last night. She had made them collect beer and pop bottles after coming home from moving sprinkler pipe. After such a long and hot day he couldn't fall asleep without a small glass of water. He had been too thirsty.

Yet he should have stayed thirsty. Even if it meant not sleeping all night. Now he had made her angry. What a stupid move. He *was* worthless. He should know better than to do something that would upset her like this. He would never learn. And now he had maybe ruined his sheets and they couldn't buy others.

Guilt washed over him as she slapped his face again. He deserved it, he knew. He only wished it didn't hurt so bad.

"But you'll learn yet, boy, mark my words. You'll learn if it kills ya."

She turned to Karl. "Pin him 'gainst the fence."

Karl grinned in understanding as she uncoiled a rubber hose.

Panic overtook David. "Wait, Ina, no! I can learn. I promise. Please! One more chance!"

"You're damn right you can learn." Ina lashed the hose across his flesh as hard as she could.

David knew it would only make things worse if he made a sound. It would only make her hit him harder and longer. It would only make Karl laugh and tease him later. But he had no choice. He screamed. The pain demanded it.

Again and again she whipped him with the rubber hose, and each time he screamed until his eyes felt they would pop. He tried to escape, even though it only made her madder. At every attempt, Karl held him roughly against the fence.

This time he couldn't count the lashes. He couldn't concentrate on anything other than staying awake. Blackness wanted to creep in on him, and he had to fight it back.

After what seemed like an eternity, she finally stopped and pulled him into the house by his ear. He prayed to God that she at least not kill him, even though he'd been a bad boy. He didn't want to die. He hoped that the punishment had finally stopped.

Ina threw him into the corner and shoved him to the floor.

"You got one hour to think about what you done," she said. "Then I have some chores for ya."

She wasn't going to kill him! David almost wanted to hug her. Instead, he merely nodded. One hour. She hardly ever let him have a full hour to rest. He had a hard time figuring out how this was punishment.

Several minutes later, someone began banging on the door as though the house were on fire. Ina looked confused. So did Karl. David wondered who would possibly slam on the door like that. He hoped they would stop soon because Ina became angrier with each knock.

"Hold your water!" she screamed at the door. The banging never stopped for a second.

Ina finally stood and rushed to the door, ready to yell at whoever made so much noise. When she threw it open, she seemed taken aback by the visitor.

Never in his life had David seen anything so unexpected. It was Mrs. O'Riley, the next door neighbor. Such a nice person. Sometimes she'd give him and Billy cookies or lemonade, and invite them to play with her own kids. He didn't think he'd ever seen her angry at anyone before.

Her face at the moment, however, was even meaner than Ina's. David couldn't believe his eyes. She looked like a grizzly about to bite somebody. Ina stood stone still.

Mrs. O'Riley spat right on Ina's face. "You filthy devil," she whispered. "I seen what you did to little Davy just now." She clenched her fists so hard they shook. "I should kill you right here for that. Before your beatings kill one of those precious boys, I oughta kill you first. I'd be doing the world a favor, and I don't think God would mind none either. Not after the way you treat those two angels."

Ina bristled. "Now listen here you little—"

Mrs. O'Riley took a menacing step forward. "If my own kids didn't need a mother, I'd have already brought my gun over and blown you back to hell where you belong." She forced a deep breath. "So because of my kids, and only because of them, I'm gonna leave you with this warning instead."

She then looked at David in such a way that he wanted to weep. Her words rocked David to the bones. The very fact that someone cared about him made him cry all over again, for some reason.

Karl looked both startled and nervous at the same time. Nobody threatened Ina. Ever.

Mrs. O'Riley turned back to Ina and took yet another step forward, forcing Ina out of the doorway. "But if I ever see you beat one of those boys like that again, my kids will have to get by without a mother. I'll go to jail after what I do to you." Mrs. O'Riley could not have looked scarier if she wanted to. David saw that she even scared Ina. This next-door neighbor, who had never even come over to ask for a cup of flour before today, had scared *Ina*.

With that, Mrs. O'Riley faced David one last time. She might as well have been looking at a dog run over by a truck. Then, she turned and left.

Ina finally found her courage and her voice. "You nosy whore!" she screamed after her. "How dare you come over and threaten me like this! If you ever get mind to do so again, remember you ain't the only one with a gun."

Mrs. O'Riley never glanced back.

"I mean it! You set foot on this property, and you're dead. I won't have you interferin' in our business!"

With a string of swear words aimed at the next door neighbor, Ina slammed the door and stormed over to David, slapping him hard in the face.

"What'd you tell that lady!"

"Nothing!" David cried out at once. He spoke the truth. David never mentioned anything to anybody about Ina, not even Dad. She scared him way too much for that.

Ina clenched her fists, ready to strike, but held back. She seemed pretty shaken up. "I don't believe you. I'm very disappointed in you, David. First of all you can't do nothin' right, no matter how hard I try to teach you and no matter how much I've done for you. Second, you try to turn our own neighbors against me with your lies."

David flinched, ready for the worst.

"Go to bed," she finally said. "I can't stand the sight of you right now. You make me sick."

"But what about—"

"No supper! Go to bed now. I can't stand the sight of you."

David blinked. He hadn't been about to ask for supper. He knew better than to ask something so stupid. It was the chores. She had never told him he could skip his chores. Billy would come home soon from collecting bottles. He'd have to do them all. He couldn't do that to his brother.

But he didn't want to make things worse than he already had. For the thousandth time, David wished he had a bedroom to go to so he wouldn't have to hear the words spoken about him. With no other options, he crawled under the blankets on his little cot, trying to hide from the sounds of Ina and Karl complaining about the neighbors and the two 'bastard children' as they always called he and Billy. They often talked about him as though he wasn't in the room.

Sleep would take awhile to come, David knew. It would be a very long time before he could forget Mrs. O'Riley's face when she looked at him like a hurt dog.

Compassion, he thought the word was. She had felt compassion for him.

So that's what it looked like.

It isn't given for us to know those rare moments when people are wide open and the lightest touch can wither or heal.

—F. Scott Fitzgerald

# Chapter 6

A knock sounded on the door while Ina sat chopping onions.
David looked up, afraid at the intrusion. Visitors almost
always meant trouble. No friends of his ever knocked on the
door, for one thing. No neighbors either.

It had been four years since Mrs. O'Riley had come over and
threatened Ina after she had whipped him with the hose. Ever
since then people had pretty much left them alone, which David
didn't mind one bit. Ina always got mad when visitors came over,
except for Karl's friends who usually walked right in without
bothering to knock anyway.

Ina crossed the kitchen and opened the door without a
word.

David couldn't believe his eyes. Of all the people in the world
he might have expect to see, this was not one of them. President
Barrett stood on the front porch, smiling up as natural as though
he stopped by all the time. What could President Barrett want?
David wondered. Peeking cautiously behind Ina, David had a
sudden and horrible thought. He hoped he hadn't done something wrong while working for President Barrett earlier in the
week and that he'd come over to talk to Ina about it.

"Hello Mrs. Briggs. How are you this evening?"

David flinched and prepared for Ina's insulting response. He
wished President Barrett hadn't come over here, whatever the reason.

He liked working for the man. They'd never worked for anyone nicer. And now Ina would probably yell at him so he wouldn't want David and Billy to help out any more.

"Fine, thanks," Ina answered. "And you?"

It was all David could do to not fall over. Ina could not have spoken nicer to President Barrett. And she didn't talk nice to anyone. Neither he or Billy ever figured out what the 'president' part of his name meant, but they figured it had to make him awfully important. President of a big company, or maybe even a city somewhere. He couldn't remember if somebody could be a president of a city or not. Maybe Ina's niceness came from him being important.

President Barrett tipped his hat. "Oh terrific, thank you. Listen, I'd first like to tell you how great a job your boys are doing. They're the hardest working kids I've ever known. You must have taught them well."

Ina didn't say anything in response.

"At any rate," he continued, "I thought I'd stop by and drop off an invitation for David and Billy to attend a social we're having at the church tomorrow night. A potluck dinner. They needn't bring anything, of course."

Now David's ears perked up. President Barrett had just invited them to a party. It'd been forever since he'd been to a party, and certainly never to a church one. He thought a church party sounded a little scary, yet definitely fun. Especially with President Barrett involved. But he quickly suppressed his hopes. *Of course Ina would never let us go,* he thought. *Not in a million—*

"Why thank you, I'm sure they'd love to go," Ina said.

David blinked. He couldn't have heard her right. No way in the world.

President Barrett smiled again. "Fantastic, it starts at seven o'clock." He looked over and saw David. "See you tomorrow!" With that, he turned and left. David could barely believe his ears.

Ina closed the door and turned around as natural as could

be, as though she always spoke that way with people. "I hope you and your brother realize this means extra chores before tomorrow night."

Extra chores. David could have kissed her. Who cared about extra chores? He was going to a party. A President Barrett party. He couldn't wait to go outside and tell Billy. President Barrett was not only the nicest man they'd ever worked for, but the nicest man they'd ever met. And he was real interesting to talk to. *And* he had invited them to his party!

Just as David thought, Billy became as excited as he was when David told him the news. That night they both had a hard time sleeping. They kept talking about the next day. Even though the next day was Saturday, one of his least favorite days of the week because of all the extra work Ina made them do, David still felt excited. It sounded like Christmas. Or at least what Christmas was supposed to sound like.

When Ina kicked them both awake at four in the morning for chores, David didn't mind in the least. The ditch-digging felt like nothing, as well as anything else Ina threw at them all day long. Her grandkids came over, normally a nuisance, but today David was in too good a mood to care. Soon they even stopped bothering to tease him or Billy, because they couldn't upset them.

"What do you think they'll have at the party?" David asked, digging another shovelful of dirt away from the drainage ditch.

Billy shrugged, pausing in his weeding for a moment to consider. "Dunno. Maybe a piñata. That could be fun. Or some clowns."

David smiled. "Do churches have clowns at their parties?"

"Well, maybe not clowns. I don't know. But I'm sure it'll be the best because President Barrett's involved. Lots of good food too. It's a dinner party."

They finished their chores well before 6:30 at night, including the woodpile. For once, Ina stayed busy enough with her grandkids that she didn't bother finding he and Billy anything else to do. In fact, she suggested they take a jar of pickles to the party and go a little early.

"There's some in the pantry."

As David stood there, dumbfounded by Ina's strange behavior, Billy ducked in and grabbed the biggest jar of pickles he could find. Then they ran off to the party, as excited as either of them had been in a long time.

The two-blocks from their house to the church flew by in what seemed like seconds. They imagined what great fun it would be to see the clowns and play the games. They tried to decide which games would be the most fun, and what desserts they might have. In all his life, David had never felt luckier.

The old church already had plenty of cars behind it when they arrived. David and Billy knew they were at least twenty minutes early, but lots of people had come even sooner to set up, it looked like. That made David even more excited. If they needed to set up this much, it had to be great. Better than great. Amazing. They smiled at each other once more and then walked through the front door, ready for the time of their lives.

When they walked through, however, some of their excitement faded.

David peeked through the big room. "There's no clowns, that's for sure."

"Nope."

There weren't any streamers either. Or balloons. In fact there weren't even many kids there. Mostly grown-ups. Only a few decorations hung around the room, and David couldn't see any games at all. No pin-the-tail on the donkey, even. A few of the grown-ups looked over at them curiously.

"Do you see President Barrett?" Billy whispered.

David looked around the room. "No. Do you think this is the right place?"

"Has to be," Billy answered. "Come on."

This was still a party, David reminded himself. And they were invited. This could still be a lot of fun. As they walked over to the table, a few more eyes turned on them. David suddenly felt very uncomfortable. He hoped President Barrett had told these people he invited him and Billy. Because they didn't look like they knew.

One man, a man David knew as Mr. Owens, began walking toward them. David barely knew Mr. Owens. At least fifty years old, he seemed nice enough normally. Not right now, though. He seemed pretty upset. Though a pretty small man compared to Dad, Mr. Owens still looked plenty mean and scary right now.

For a few moments Mr. Owens stood there not saying anything, frowning down on David and Billy. David's throat tightened and face reddened. He hoped they hadn't done anything bad. This man was staring at them like they had broken some serious rule. David quickly glanced behind him to see if they had tracked any mud in on the floor.

The man pointed to what Billy held in his hands, and leaned in. He cleared his throat and spoke loudly. "So. You two think you can mooch a meal off of that jar of pickles."

The entire room fell silent as the adults each in turn gave disapproving stares to the two brothers.

David's heart broke at the accusation. Everyone in the room looked at them the same way as Mr. Owens. As though he and Billy were thieves. Guilt and shame flooded into him as he realized they had made a terrible, terrible mistake in coming.

Without a word, he and Billy turned and snuck out of the party, more ashamed than they'd ever felt in their entire lives. This was all his fault. He should have known better than to come to a fancy party like that with only a jar of pickles. Soon President Barrett would hear about it and get angry. He'd be embarrassed for even inviting them. David wanted to cry, but wouldn't let himself.

He and Billy walked far enough away from the church to be out of sight before sinking down on the grass.

"Here," Billy said, shoving over the jar of pickles. "I don't want any. I'm going for a walk."

With that, Billy stormed off. David sat quietly for a few minutes before popping open the jar of pickles and eating them, more for something to do than because of hunger. He needed to keep his mind off of what had just happened. In all the whole community, only one person had ever treated them nicely. And with one single mistake, he and Billy had certainly disappointed that one person.

At least President Barrett wasn't there to see what happened. If he had seen them bring in such a stupid dinner item, he would have scowled at them too. But he'd hear about it soon enough. And then he'd never talk to them again.

Cramming down another pickle, David took a deep breath to try and calm himself.

Hot tears fought their way to David's eyes, but he held them back. He would not cry. Not over this. Besides, it wasn't such a big deal. It got him away from Ina for awhile. And the party didn't have clowns or balloons or anything fun anyway. It would have been a waste of time. In fact, this was the best thing that could have happened. Not only did he get to stay away from Ina, he didn't have to sit through some boring party.

David pushed back another wave of tears. "Stop it," he told himself. "No crying." That would be stupid. Especially over something so small as a dumb grown-up party.

He figured he probably needed a walk too. Stuffing the rest of the pickles in his mouth, he poured out the juice before putting the lid back on. Ina would want the jar back. He began walking down the street, trying to ignore the pounding in his chest.

He hadn't been gone from home very long yet. Maybe he could sneak down to the canal and go swimming. No, swimming didn't sound fun either. Maybe he could go and grab a bite to eat at Jimmy's house. He had at least an hour left before he'd have to go home, after all.

But David didn't want to see Jimmy either right then. Jimmy talked too much. In fact, he didn't want to see anyone. He wanted to be alone. It sounded better and better after all that he didn't have to suffer through a bunch of grown-ups having dinner or whatever they were doing.

David turned and faced the brick side wall of the hardware store. Without thinking, he hurled the empty glass jar at the wall as hard as he could. It shattered into a thousand pieces. David stood there for a moment watching the glass settle to the ground before realizing what a stupid thing he had just done. Ina would be really upset over that.

So what? David decided. She could buy another one. She could use the lunch money she took from him and Billy and buy another five of them if she wanted. It was only a jar.

He'd had enough walking. It was time to go home. He didn't want anything but sleep. If Ina tried to make him do any chores, he'd tell her to go jump in the lake. He had already done enough chores today. Her grandkids could help, if she needed them to. They were always getting the treats and making a mess. Let them clean up for once. He only wanted to go home and forget that this day ever happened.

As he walked home, he wondered when Billy would come back. Billy had looked pretty upset. Now that he'd had some time to think about it, David didn't know why his brother took it so hard. It didn't mean anything.

He opened the door and walked over to his cot in the corner without once looking at Ina or her annoying grandkids.

Ina glanced over at him. "Where's your brother?"

"I don't know," David spat back.

"You don't know?" she asked, her voice rising.

"No, I don't. And if you want to find him, why don't you take your four little *brats* with you and find him yourself. I'm going to sleep."

He couldn't believe he'd said that. He never said things like that to Ina. Karl got up off the couch, ready to help Ina if needed.

"Excuse me?" Ina asked. Danger laced her words.

"Beat him gramma!" one of them called out. "Use a belt this time!"

Dread gripped David, but he refused to give into it. Karl walked over and gripped David like a rag doll. Karl had been hitting the gym more than usual lately and had arms like a truck.

David watched Ina as she got out of the chair. He knew what

would come next. And he also knew he had brought this one on himself. Again. "Not in front of the kids," he begged.

She laughed. "You mean my brats? I think they'll be all right." The grandkids laughed. She took a belt from one of them and looked to Karl. "Take his shirt off." She turned back to David. "The bible says that liars and disobedient children are gonna go to Hell, David. And I don't want that to happen to you, no matter what you think. Do you really want to burn and burn in fire and brimstone forever?"

David didn't say anything. It never mattered once she got like this.

"And so, since I don't want you to burn in Hell, I've got to make a good boy out of you yet."

The grandkids whooped and laughed. David felt hot shame wash over him as his stepbrother wrenched off his shirt. He had been beaten so many times in his life he couldn't keep count, but he didn't want to have her grandkids laughing and teasing him the whole time. "Please, Ina, not in front—"

She brought the belt across his flesh in a stinging lash. The grandkids laughed as she whipped him again and again. David was used to the pain, but the laughter cut deeper. He was a freak show. A clown, even.

Ina whipped harder and harder until the pain itself finally overrode the embarrassment. He broke down crying and begged her to stop. This only made the grandkids laugh more. David thrashed so hard against Karl's grip that he thought his arms would break but Karl never let go.

David sobbed as Ina continued, her energy and determination far from spent. He thought he might pass out. She hadn't beat him this bad in years. And all the while, the grandchildren giggled with delight.

With all the sounds of laughter and of his own crying, he couldn't hear much else. Finally Ina said something David couldn't make out and Karl threw him down on the floor. David didn't know if they were planning anything worse for him, but he didn't want to wait around and find out.

He grabbed his shirt off the floor and ran out the door with the sounds of Ina's grandchildren's teasing and mocking fading behind him. David ran down along the canal, putting his shirt on over the bleeding welts that were already forming. Dad wasn't home of course, but maybe he would come back tonight. There was always a chance.

After he felt sure Ina couldn't see him anymore, David crossed the canal and went to the store not far from his house. He went to his own little safe haven under the canopy of the store and in the shadows where nobody could see him. Here he had come countless times during the years to spy on his own house until Dad got home. Close enough to see when Dad would arrive but far enough, and hidden enough, that Ina could never see him there. This was the one place in the world where he felt safe.

No sooner did he enter his secret place than David dropped to his knees and cried violently. The harder he tried to regain composure, the worse he sobbed. He felt foolish but couldn't stop it. In his mind he could see the look of disapproval that Mr. Owens and everybody else in the church had given him. He and Billy had only gone in the first place because President Barrett had asked them to come. Why did the grown-ups have to act so mad, even if what he and Billy brought wasn't good enough?

He saw as well the laughing faces of Ina's grandchildren. He could hear their taunting voices. For twenty minutes he cried as hard as he ever had in his life. No matter how hard he tried to suppress the tears, they poured out all the stronger. It got so he could hardly breath. He remembered how she beat him harder and harder the whole time. For not the first time he feared she would some day snap completely and kill him in one of the beatings.

Nearly a half hour after he arrived, he could finally draw an even breath. He looked up to the stars, where he thought God lived. "Dear God," he began. "Please don't let her kill me. Even if I'm bad. Don't let her beat me to death. I . . . I can do better. I can. But I don't want to die."

A few minutes passed by as he looked at the empty stars. He

felt, as always, a very quiet whisper in his heart that someone somewhere loved him. That whisper felt really small right now, but David clung to it nevertheless. "I need strength, God. I know now that I'm not good enough to go mix with the church people, and I'm sorry for trying, but please make me strong enough that Ina won't kill me."

He took a deep breath before finishing. "Billy needs me, and I need him. Help keep us both alive, dear God. Amen."

Billy came home an hour later and, as far as David could tell from his viewpoint under the canopy, Ina didn't whip him. Good, he thought. No reason they both needed to get beaten after such a horrible night.

He waited and waited for Dad to come home and he never did. Long after all the lights went out, David walked home and tiptoed through the door without making a sound. Tomorrow morning Ina would probably take it out on him for coming in so late, but he didn't want to deal with her again so soon. He didn't think he could.

He snuck over to his cot undetected and lay down.

"Where you been?" Billy whispered.

"At the store, waitin' for Dad."

Billy lay in silence for a minute. "That bad, huh?"

David didn't have to ask what Billy meant. When she beat either of them bad enough, they usually disappeared for awhile. David always went to the same spot by the store.

It took a moment for David to reply. "Yeah. Pretty bad."

"That's the last one of those parties I'm ever going to," Billy whispered.

"Same here," David said fervently.

As he struggled to fall asleep, the one thing that burned in David's memory over and over again was that mean look from all the grown-ups in the room when Mr. Owens scolded them. He and Billy had been foolish to go, but they would at least remember the lesson. He knew better than to make that mistake again.

There are few nudities so objectionable as the naked truth.

—Agnes Repplier

# Chapter 7

A strong breeze whipped across David's face as he walked home from the Wellington's farm. The golden, fall-colored hills should have looked beautiful, but he felt too exhausted to notice. Billy had doubled back for some schoolwork he'd left behind before going home. David had left his own books back at school as well, but he did so on purpose. He had no intention of doing any homework.

Not for the first time, he wondered if he'd pass the seventh grade. His teachers, especially Mr. Sanderson, said he wouldn't if he didn't show up more often. It's not like it mattered, though. He wouldn't be alive long enough to worry about college, a career, or anything like that. He knew that much at least. He was stupid, worthless, and nobody loved him—not even his own mom—and he couldn't do anything right. How could he possibly live long enough to bother "planning for the future" like Mr. Sanderson always told him to do? What a joke.

Though Dad wouldn't come home until late tonight, Ina was gone working at the potato warehouse too, which kinda made up for it. David liked this time of year for that reason. With Ina working, he didn't have to endure her yelling and constant chores as much. Even with her gone, however, Karl tried to take up the slack. And with as huge as Karl had become, still hitting the weights all the time like he did, David didn't know who was worse between the two of them.

When he got home he opened the front door quietly, ready to crash under his cot. He'd been up since three in the morning and felt more tired than usual. He wanted nothing else but to fall asleep, even though light still shone outside. Maybe he had hit a growth spurt like Billy had recently and needed more sleep than usual. Whatever the reason, David had been dead tired the past few weeks. At least with Ina gone he could catch up a little on some sleep. He lay down on top of the cot, ready to give in to deep slumber. He'd roll under the cot when Billy showed up and needed his spot on top.

Karl called over from the couch. "Hey, Davey," David's insides churned at the voice. "Ain't it a little early for bed? I'm sure Mom's got something for you to do."

"She didn't give me anything," David said, irritated. He hated when Karl tried to give him chores. "I'm tired and going to sleep."

"Well maybe I got some chores for you, then," Karl said. "Go over to the Johnsons and borrow me a marble. I'm bored."

"Get it yourself," David said without thinking.

For a few moments Karl said nothing. David realized suddenly that he had never spoken back to Karl before. Not even over something small like this.

"Excuse me?" Karl asked.

"I said, get it yourself." David repeated, too exhausted for this. He didn't care if Karl got angry over it, he would not walk over to his neighbor's house and ask for a stupid marble. He hated listening to Karl. Karl always bossed him around like his stepmother did. He was sick of listening to him. Sick of everything. He wanted nothing but sleep. He closed his eyes and thought he might fall asleep in seconds.

Through the haze of near sleep David could hear Karl stand up and walk over to his cot. He opened his eyes just in time to see his stepbrother's hand fly downward before ending in a stinging slap across his jaw. Fatigue vanished immediately as he saw his stepbrother staring down at him.

"Now," Karl whispered, ugly anger rising on his face."I said to go fetch me a marble. Go get it."

David tightened his fists. Things never changed around here. Move the woodpile. Dig the ditches. Go earn money, even if it's three o'clock in the morning. It was one thing to take all of that from Ina. Dad married her and that sort of made her his mom. But not Karl. Karl had never been anything but a mean, spoiled brat of an older stepbrother. All the years that David had been pushed around came swirling up at once. His body ached with exhaustion. Karl didn't need that marble. He just wanted to push David around. Like always.

David finally stood up from the cot and met his stepbrothers stare. "I said no." He braced himself for Karl's reaction. But he didn't care at this point. A strange and sudden resolve settled over him. He had let Karl push him around for the last time.

Karl walked away without a sound and left the house. David let out a sigh of relief. It had worked! He stood up to Karl for the first time in his life and it had worked. Why hadn't he done so sooner?

The door swung open with a crash and Karl stormed back into the house, this time carrying a double-barreled shotgun. David's mouth dropped as Karl raised the gun and pointed it straight at his face.

"I'm giving you one last chance, maggot," Karl hissed. "You seem to be forgettin' something. You're worthless. You're nobody. So when I say you do something, you listen and that's it." Karl cocked the gun. "Now you go get me a marble, or I pull the trigger."

This was it, David realized. All the pain and suffering would finally end. This was how he would die. He knew he wouldn't have to worry about his future, to say nothing about the seventh grade. Because no way would he give in to Karl any more. Not now, not ever. He'd sooner die than do what Karl told him to.

"Go ahead and shoot," David said.

David honestly believed Karl would pull the trigger. He

looked that mad. But he didn't. He threw the gun down and balled his hands into fists. Karl's 240 pounds of solid muscle ended in hands of iron. As hard as he could, Karl hauled back and slammed his fist square into David's face.

One punch knocked him to the floor. David couldn't believe the explosion of pain in his head. From Ina's treatment to him through the years, he certainly knew a lot about pain. He thought he could handle plenty of it. Now, however, he had a whole new definition as Karl began screaming and kicking David over and over with steel-toed boots.

Maybe Karl intended to kill him after all, only not with a gun. David screamed involuntarily at the anguish that washed over him from the attacks.

Without mercy, Karl jumped on top of David and pounded his fists time and again on David's face and neck. His vision blurred in a cloud of red. Blackness infringed on the edges of his sight. Karl acted in absolute rage.

David sobbed and pleaded for him to stop, but it did no good. Karl hauled David to his feet and pinned him up against a wall with one arm and rained showers of bloody-knuckled punches with the other. All the while he kept on screaming, screaming, screaming.

"You filthy bastard!" Karl howled. "Who do you think you are?"

But David could barely hear him let alone answer. He could feel himself dying inside. Karl was killing him a piece at a time. Every time the muscular giant punched him he felt something else break within. At first he tried to defend himself, but to no avail. Karl seemed bent on his total destruction, with David powerless to stop him. For a brief moment David thought of Dad, wishing him home now more than ever. David didn't want to die like this without saying goodbye to him. Or maybe taking another fishing trip or two with him. He loved him.

Karl elbowed him across the jaw, shattering any thoughts of future memories. Then David felt his legs being kicked again by steel-toe boots. He couldn't stand up any longer, but Karl wouldn't let him fall.

*Please God,* David pleaded, *please just let me die. I can't take this any more.*

About that time the blackness washed over him.

At first, when David regained consciousness, he really believed he had died. That all changed, however, when he tried to move and the pain taught him otherwise. Dead people didn't feel pain, he reasoned. David lay on his cot, obviously alive, but thought every bone in his body must've been broken. He tentatively reached his face and felt it sticky with blood. Even his hair was matted with it.

Karl's voice carried over to him. "That should teach ya to listen, you worthless dog."

Listen? Listen to what. David tried to remember what had happened but he couldn't. He only knew that if he tried to move he would scream out in pain. What had he done to Karl to upset him?

A marble. Hazy memories drifted back to him bits at a time. This had all happened because he told Karl he wouldn't get a marble, and Karl had killed him for it. Even if David wasn't dead, it couldn't be much longer before his body gave out. Not dead yet, but *dying* for certain. Probably any minute. He wished it would happen soon and end this hurting.

The door swung open and David lifted his head feebly to see who came in.

"Hey David, I thought you'd forget your—"

It was Billy. Billy dropped whatever he had been holding, *books,* David thought, and rushed over to him.

"Wh-what happened to you?" Billy asked. David had been beat plenty of times over the years. Plenty. He and Billy had seen each other go through seven stages of hell from leather belts to willows, rubber hoses, and even once with a bull whip. But he had never seen Billy look at him like that before.

Karl answered Billy's question for him. "Little punk needed a lesson," he said smugly. David saw Billy's face go taut, then shake with rage. Dread filled David as he realized what Billy would do next. He knew that look in his brother and knew also that in this instance it would be suicide if he acted on it.

"Billy, no. Wait . . . "

"That's it," Billy said, standing and facing Karl with clenched fists. There could be no mistaking Billy's intentions.

David could hardly breath as he watched his brother stand there, his chest heaving in fury. He'd seen Billy whip a kid once and still remembered how scary the fight had been to watch. When Billy got like that, he didn't hardly look like a person anymore. More like an animal.

Even so, David knew that Billy's anger would be no match for Karl's raw size. Karl was still three years older and much bigger than Billy. David watched in apprehension, anxiety crushing him as he watched the events unfold. He couldn't bear it if Karl killed Billy on account of him.

Karl jumped up off the couch and grabbed a broom, holding it like a baseball bat. "You want a piece of me too?" he screamed.

Billy never wavered. David doubted if he even saw the broom. His brother charged with such speed that Karl barely had time to swing the broom handle. The wooden shaft broke across Billy's arm, but if it hurt him he didn't show it. He crashed into Karl and began pummeling Karl's face with fists and muscles forged from a lifetime of hard labor. David couldn't believe what he saw. For the first time in his life, and in the unlikeliest of circumstances, he saw fear on Karl's face. Very real fear.

Anger quickly replaced the fear, however. Obviously caught off guard, Karl quickly recovered. He picked Billy up and threw him away, squaring off to throw some punches of his own. David knew with dreadful certainty that those first few punches were the only ones Billy would get a chance to throw.

But what happened next could not have taken David more by surprise. Billy rebounded like a cat and kicked Karl's feet out from underneath him. No concern for his own safety, Billy tumbled down on top, crashing into the wall as he gripped Karl by the throat. David managed to sit up and watch. He couldn't believe his eyes.

With one hand, Billy held Karl's throat to the floor, and with the other he struck any part of Karl's body he could find exposed. Karl cried out in pain over and over again, but Billy never stopped.

Finally, Karl's superior size paid off and he flung Billy free. He stood up and landed a few hits before Billy could fully recover. The punches might as well have been flies biting at Billy for all the effect they had. His brother never flinched. Karl must have noticed as much too because he scrambled over the table and grabbed a chair. Not to use as a weapon, but simply to place between himself and Billy.

Billy shrieked and charged Karl once more, full speed. He batted the chair out of the way with one arm and rammed his other shoulder into Karl's chest so hard he lifted him clear off the ground and into the front door. With a splintering crack the door burst off its hinges as the two fighters tumbled through.

Though his head seemed like it would explode from doing so, David staggered to his feet and hobbled over to the empty doorway to watch. Billy had straddled a screaming Karl and was pounding punch after frenzied punch down on his bloodied face.

Karl had long since stopped fighting and only tried to protect himself. David's world had turned upside down. He couldn't believe the sight in front of him: Karl screaming out for mercy and Billy finally unleashing years of built up anger for the injustices he and David both had endured.

How many times had Karl held them for Ina while she whipped them senseless? How many times had Karl himself beaten them? How many times had Ina taken his side over theirs, no matter how ridiculous the situation? Or stolen their money to give to Karl?

Everything had gone backwards and inside out all at once.

Finally, Billy vented enough of his anger to stop punching. He got up on one knee and said something to Karl that

David didn't hear from the broken doorway. Once Billy stood up and released his grip, Karl immediately ran away but not before Billy could yell one more threat at him that David heard perfectly clear.

"And if you touch him again, I'll kill ya!"

Ina had come home before Dad that night, but David had no clue what she thought of the mess inside, or of Karl. David was hiding. He knew Dad would be home for sure that night, and he didn't want to be around Karl until Dad saw what he had done.

Even though Billy had walloped Karl, David knew better than to think Ina would leave it at that. Or that Karl wouldn't try and get his revenge. In fact, he now feared Karl more than ever. It didn't take a genius to realize that Billy had whipped him good, but Karl was the type of person who found ways to get even one way or another.

David still felt so much pain he could hardly think straight. He caught a glimpse of himself in a mirror earlier and didn't recognize his own face. His lips were swollen and cracked beyond belief. Dried blood covered his whole face. His eyes were deep black and puffy. His skull was cracked slightly, and still bled if he moved too much. Dark bruises covered his legs and chest.

Normally he would have gone to his secret place by the store, but that sounded too far to travel tonight. He decided to simply lay in the dry canal bed until Dad came home. Billy hadn't wanted David to leave the house injured like that, but David figured it would only be worse if Karl came back angrier than ever and decided to finish what he'd started and beat him again.

Karl had come home shortly after Ina. Billy, however, stayed long gone. After taking care of David as best he could, Billy stormed off for a walk, afraid that if he didn't cool down himself he might do something he'd regret later. For years now, Billy had developed the habit of going for long walks when he needed to calm down. And in his whole life David had never seen Billy so angry. He didn't expect him back any time soon.

Several hours passed before Dad finally showed up. David watched as Dad eyed the broken front door with confusion before entering the house. Climbing out of the ditch brought all of his injuries back to the surface, but he managed. No matter how angry Karl might be, Dad would be there to protect him.

Hobbling over to the house took enormous effort.

He caught a glimpse of his reflection in the window. His face had swollen even worse, if possible. He looked like an entirely different person. With a final deep breath, he walked through the splintered doorway. Dad turned around to say hello and turned sickly white at seeing his bloodied and broken son.

"David! What happened to you?" Dad's face continued to drain of color as his eyes widened. Karl backed into the corner, warning David with his eyes not to say anything.

For a moment David had second thoughts, but decided he couldn't back down now. "Karl wanted me to get him something from the Johnsons" he spit out, "and I said no."

Color flashed back into Dad's face as he absorbed the words. "You mean to say that Karl did this to you?" Dad's voice had turned so dangerous David didn't know what to think. He had never seen Dad so intense before. All he could do to answer was barely nod his head.

Dad swung around and stared Karl down like a cockroach he intended to crush. Karl stood up as well, not the least bit afraid. David watched as Karl lunged forward and took the first swing. Of all the dumb things David had seen Karl do, this was by far the stupidest. Dad had once been a professional boxer. Everybody in town knew Dad as the toughest guy around. Karl wouldn't have a prayer.

Before Karl could even land that first punch, Dad reached out and picked him up like a piece of straw, turned him upside down, and bashed his head on the floor a couple times. He threw him to the ground like a rag doll and moved to lay into him again. This time, however, Karl scrambled out of the way and ran out of the house.

When David should have been happy seeing Karl get his lickings twice in one day, he all of a sudden felt terrible. Anxiety gripped his throat so tight he could barely breath. Dad stood there yelling at Ina about her son, the veins bulging at his neck. David couldn't pinpoint the problem. Something was wrong. Horribly wrong.

And in the next instant he saw what.

"Dad look out!" he screamed. "Karl's got a gun!"

The night exploded with sound as Karl fired his OTT 6 from outside the house window. Dad dove to the floor barely in time. The bullets shattered into the cabinets behind them. Karl reloaded.

Those weren't meant to be warning shots, David knew. Karl was actually trying to kill them.

"Get down!" Dad screamed to David. David threw himself to the floor, heedless of the pain it caused him. Karl fired again into the house, narrowly missing them.

Karl reloaded. "You think you can whip me, old man?" He used the butt of the gun to break through the rest of the window, stuck the barrel of his gun inside, and aimed again. "Think again!" Karl pulled the trigger as Dad rolled closer to the window. Bright flashes of light accompanied the blast. The bullets narrowly missed. Dad jumped to his feet and lurched for the gun, but Karl jerked back in time.

Without hesitation, Dad charged out the front door ready to tackle Karl. Karl had no time to reload and obviously had no intentions of staying and fighting. For the second time that day Karl ran off into the night.

David hobbled out in the front yard to check on Dad, who chased Karl clear to the end of the block before finally stopping. David looked into the house again. No doubt about it, those bullets had been meant for Dad's head and chest. Karl had tried to murder Dad. A chill ran through David as he realized how close he had come to losing his dad.

Before returning, Dad asked one of the neighbors who had come out to call the police. David watched him walk the rest of the way. His fists were clenched tight enough to crush bricks. Dad had never been so angry before.

He walked past David and into the house without saying a word. Ina sat deathly afraid, crouching in the corner like a trapped mouse. David realized again how Dad really had no clue at all what had ever gone on here at home. He loved his boys, but he never stayed around enough to understand how Ina and Karl actually treated them. Now, however, Dad had finally figured out a little bit of it the hard way.

With one glance at Ina, and two simple words, David's world turned upside down again.

"We're through," Dad said.

"Hey, David!" a familiar voice sounded. "How did you know we were going to be here today?"

David turned in confusion. Mr. Sanderson smiled up at him for an instant, and then cringed.

"Whoa! What happened to you? Did you get in a bike accident?"

"Something like that," David answered, uncertainty gnawing at him. Why would Mr. Sanderson be at the courthouse instead of school? What was going on?

Then he saw Kirk Mellings and Cindy Croft come in the back door as well. Followed by Mark Young and several others from his class.

David's heart plummeted. No. Not that.

"So anyway," Mr. Sanderson continued, "I haven't seen you at school for awhile so I didn't get a chance to tell you about the field trip. Somebody must have told you, though, that's great! You'll learn a lot here today."

Once he heard Mr. Sanderson confirm his worst fears, David knew he had to get out of the building. He didn't care if somebody arrested him for it. The courtroom now held at least twenty of his schoolmates. He wouldn't let them hear all these horrible details from his life. They already thought he was a freak.

Mr. Sanderson turned around and began explaining to the students walking in about the various aspects of the courtroom and what to expect during a court case. David could take no more. He'd rather land in jail than talk about what had happened to him in front of his class. Time to go.

He stood up, covering his face as best he could, and turned to leave the room when a loud voice called out.

"All rise!"

David closed his eyes in horror. Too late.

"You may be seated," the judge said.

For a few moments David remained standing, uncertain what to do. The judge shuffled his papers. This was a different judge than from the last time he had been here, but he looked every bit as intimidating.

"David Briggs, please take the stand," the judge called out.

A few of his classmates started whispering in confusion upon hearing and recognizing his name. They hadn't noticed him there yet. Mr. Sanderson looked at him with pity as realization dawned on the teacher.

While walking to the stand, David felt like the freak he was. Every eye in the room locked on him. He could hear several of the kids laughing while others gasped at how ugly his face looked. He knew the terrible bruising and swelling had not improved much since the fight with Karl three days ago.

The judge cleared his throat and took a sip of water. "Please tell me in your own words, son, what happened last Tuesday."

Even though he looked down at the floor, David knew everyone in the room stared at him all the same. His face flushed with shame, but he had no choice. He had to answer the judge or bad things would happen.

As he began relating the events of that day, the world around him became smaller and smaller. Everything that ever mattered outside the courtroom faded from existence. He could barely even think about what he told the judge.

The one thing that overwhelmed his mind more than anything else were the gasps and shocked whispers from his classmates as they watched and listened to the freak on display. It was as though he stood stripped bare in front of the world. Cold, naked, and ashamed.

Ina had been right after all. He *was* worthless. A nobody. A monster. Apparently it wasn't enough that he realize it himself. Somebody somewhere decided to shine a spotlight on him so that everybody else would know it too.

Life would never be the same after today. As distant as his classmates had been before now, he knew that from this day forward they would even step off the sidewalk if only to avoid being near him. The truth was out. They knew his dark secrets.

Resigned to the fact that the damage had already been done, David patiently answered the judge's questions. Soon he could go home, wherever that might be.

Soon the freak show would be over.

Alice huddled in her chair, looking like she had seen a ghost.

"Are you all right?" David asked softly.

She shook herself out of the fog she had slipped into. "That must have been awful. Having to talk about such horrible things in front of your school."

"Yes, awful. Lonely, scary, and a hundred other things. But the true low point was actually before any of that happened. You asked earlier if I have ever stared death square in the face and invited it in the door. The moment Karl pointed the gun at me and I realized I didn't care if he pulled the trigger, I did just that. Fortunately for me, death didn't step across the threshold."

Alice slumped a little further in her chair, deep in thought.

"It's a tragic day indeed when somebody decides the hardships of life outweigh the reasons to go on." David took a slow breath, emotion causing his voice to catch. He had said all he could for one day, and reasoned that Alice couldn't listen to much more in one setting anyhow.

Looking over at her slender frame, the reasoning became perfectly clear as to why he had needed to share that particular story. Alice was feeling now how he had felt those many years ago. Somebody had a gun aimed right to her chest and she honestly didn't care if it fired or not.

But she needed to care, and quick.

"I'd better be going. Can I get you anything?" He tried to lighten the mood a bit. "My wife's a fantastic cook. I could bring you her lasagna if you'd like. It's got to taste better than whatever they serve around here."

She shook her head again. "Thank you, though."

David cleared his throat. "We're not done. There's more you need to hear. Only not tonight."

"You know where to find me," she said, apparently lost in thought.

"Good night, then. And remember . . . it really does get better. I can't tell you how glad I am now that he didn't pull that trigger after all."

Alice nodded once more, but her carefully guarded thoughts he had no way of knowing. David sent another silent prayer for guidance heavenward and then left the room without another word.

No act of kindness, no matter how small, is ever wasted.

—Aesop

# Chapter 8

When Alice answered the door this time, David was pleased to see a friendly face looking back at him for a change.

"Hello, David," she said. "Good to see you."

*That's certainly progress,* David thought. He didn't have to fight off any hostilities for the first ten minutes or so. "Alice, would you mind if we went on a walk today? I think some fresh air could do us both some good."

He left unsaid the destination to which they would be walking.

Alice appeared more than happy to leave the halfway house and grabbed her coat. The cold weather outside still retained a certain bite, but at least the sunny day took off the edge a little. The string of storms in this past couple of weeks had left quite the oppressive feeling in the air. Once the holidays passed, David knew, most people were ready for warm weather. Though it still felt like December, the first calendar day of spring was actually only two days away.

"So how's your family, David?"

"Oh, fine. Fine. We keep plenty busy this time of year."

They walked down the hallway and descended the stairs to the lobby in silence. *Alice was conducting herself pleasantly enough,* David thought, but something remained on her mind. He wondered what.

The attendant never looked up from his post. David shook his head, not bothering to bring up the hundred accusatory remarks always on the tip of his tongue when he visited this building. With more than a small amount of restraint, David led Alice out of the building without saying a word to the man.

The brisk air was invigorating, though they had to squint against the brightness of the sunlight on the snow. The sun had almost set, but still cast enough light to reflect in a million different angles off the crystalline ground cover and nearly blind them in the process.

David promptly turned left once they reached the sidewalk. Fortunately, Alice didn't ask where they were going and simply followed.

He asked a few questions about her thoughts on the weather, how she was doing in general and such, and she answered them but stayed distant and reserved on the whole.

After a few blocks, however, she finally ventured to change the course of conversation.

"David, I don't mean to sound unkind or ungrateful," she gripped his shoulder firmly to emphasize her words, "but I honestly don't understand why you are spending this time with me or telling me about such painful memories." She released the grip on his shoulder and looked down at the ground.

Nodding, David waited patiently for her to go on. He could tell she didn't expect him to answer quite yet.

"I mean, it must be hard for you to bring all this up. And you don't even know me. Your life has obviously been difficult. What it boils down to I guess is that I don't know why you're bothering. I don't deserve the effort."

She looked into his eyes for a brief moment and then back at the ground.

He took a moment to collect his thoughts. "Alice, I think you know why I tell you these things. You need to understand that people can get better and that hard times need not be permanent. Good comes at the other end. And happiness."

"Yes, I can see that you've found it," she replied. "But I know

I won't. I'm not strong like you. I'm not anywhere near that strong. I'd have cracked the first year." She cleared her throat, fighting back emotion. "I'm just not worth your efforts, David. When Lily died, my will to live died with her. I'm afraid I have nothing left to give."

David wanted to say so many things to Alice right then, starting with the fact that she was so young and her whole life still lay ahead of her. Also that she clearly couldn't see past the immediacy of the moment, but if she simply tried she would.

Instead, he said nothing. Deep down he knew that the time had not yet come for such words. Anything he might say in that regard she would likely shoot down or dismiss.

They had business elsewhere first. Alice said nothing as they continued walking.

Only when they reached their destination and David turned to enter the building he had taken them to did Alice snap out of her internal haze.

"What are we doing here?"

"This is a rest home," David answered. "I thought we should pay a visit."

Alice shuddered. "I'd rather not."

"Why is that?"

For a few moments she merely stood there, looking thoroughly distressed. "Because I already feel bad enough about myself when I hear what you went through. I . . . I don't think I could take seeing all the people suffering in here."

David smiled. "Please trust me. You have this all wrong."

He gestured to the door and she reluctantly followed. The well-lit hallways inside the hospital struck quite the contrast to the building they'd left behind.

"Hello, Bishop!" one of the nurses called over. "How are you today?"

"Great, thank you. I've brought someone with me tonight. I'd like you to meet Alice Chambers." Alice extended her hand in greeting. "Alice would like to play a little piano music for the residents, if that's all right."

The nurse's eyes brightened considerably, but Alice turned deathly pale. David hated to shove Alice into this without any warning, but he knew he could never have talked her into it otherwise.

"Oh that's marvelous!" the nurse squealed. "Please, come this way. They'll be so glad to hear some music."

The nurse hustled off and Alice leaned in with an urgent whisper.

"David! I can't! I haven't played in years. Not since Lily . . . I couldn't possibly."

"Chopsticks will be fine," David answered. "The rest home gets plenty of volunteers for board game nights, dance instruction, and so forth but rarely musicians. Anything will do."

As she turned in exasperation to follow the excited nurse, David couldn't repress a smile. If nothing else, the nurse gathering patients along the way created quite the stir. Likely quite a crowd would get together.

The nurse led the two of them into an assembly room where some thirty or forty gray-haired residents were gathered, with others streaming in. She announced Alice as a musician and instantly received enthusiastic applause. Alice looked ready to melt into the floor. She seemed beyond embarrassed. Mortified. Terrified.

*Good,* David thought. She had been getting a little too melancholy for her own good lately. Nothing like a little white-hot fear to shake things up a bit. He only hoped the experience would prove more than just fearful. An adventure, perhaps. She could certainly use one.

Alice sat at the baby grand piano and stared at the keys. She looked like a toddler trying to comprehend a college dictionary. David gulped in apprehension. Maybe this hadn't been such a good idea after all.

She stared at the instrument for a full minute in complete silence. Even the rest home tenants, an enormously supportive crowd, began whispering to one another and wondering aloud at the problem. Soon some of the tenants turned back to their games.

*Please,* David prayed, *let her play.*

Alice continued to stare with seeming incomprehension at the piano.

A stab of panic chilled David's blood. This was not going well at all. He had brought her too soon. There would be no undoing the damage he had caused today. Alice continued regarding the keys as one would a poisonous snake.

The prolonged and awkward silence finally took its toll on David. He had to get her out of here. He had been mistaken to bring her here. Grossly mistaken.

As he began standing up to go retrieve Alice, a single note rang out from the piano. David paused. Had that been an accident? Had her hand merely dropped? He waited to hear more.

Another note rang out, and then another. David could scarcely contain his relief. She was playing a song. No matter how simple or choppy it may be, she was playing. He wanted to shout for joy.

The few residents that had turned away now paid attention once more.

Alice's hands traveled over the keyboard rigidly and stiff. She hit the keys without any grace or rhythm. The notes were forced out without benefit of any apparent musicianship or love for the craft. David didn't recognize the melody, nor did he much care for it. Alice looked as though she were in physical pain as she played. Each note seemed to exact a cost from her and was doled out begrudgingly. He never knew playing an instrument could be such an unpleasant experience.

He longed for the ordeal to end.

Some of the tenants eyed her curiously. Alice's face remained a visage of near-torture. Clearly this piano recital fell outside the realm of anything they had witnessed before.

David's throat constricted in pain as he watched her. He felt like he had shoved one of his own children into the harsh realities of the world before they were ready for them. He might as well have thrown her to the wolves. The experience clearly would do more harm than good.

Her song begun, he had no choice but to wait and listen until she finished.

The notes began flowing noticeably smoother, to David's relief. At least she appeared to have fallen into some form of rhythm. Soon she would finish the song and he would whisk her out of this room, begging her forgiveness for—

David was stunned. Alice's face began transforming before his eyes. The mask of pain she wore might as well have crumbled to dust in that very room. Her countenance began to shine with something pure, something full of love and passion.

As her face changed, so did the song. Her hands, scant moments ago blunt and stiff instruments over the keys, became fluid. Graceful. Powerful. The melody took on a life of its own, rising and falling in response to some giantess of emotion within Alice that literally demanded release through the music.

Every eye in the room stayed absolutely riveted. Not a sound rose in the vicinity beyond that of her playing. People tiptoed into the room from all throughout the building, lured by the powerful melody yet careful not to detract from it. David could scarcely breath. He had heard music of all kinds throughout his life. Music had many times been powerful, moving, and spiritual for him.

This was something on a different level altogether.

The woman at the piano this night bared her soul with this music in a way he had not believed possible. And in that soul for all to see the music revealed love, goodness, kindness, and tremendous inner beauty. Her hands flew over the keyboard as if they had never performed any other function. She didn't miss a single note. It wouldn't have been possible.

Alice wept soundlessly while playing, lost to anything but the music. Tears slid down the faces of men and women alike throughout the room, David among them. The song remained unfamiliar to him but sounded as though it belonged in the heavens, or as though it came from there directly at this moment, given to Alice in her time of need.

Time slipped away in the spell of her music. Ten minutes,

maybe twenty passed and David would not have known the difference. When at last Alice finished her song, she did so with a finesse that chilled every heart in the building. No one clapped. No one made a sound.

David knew their refraining had nothing whatsoever to do with a lack of appreciation. Applause would have ruined that moment.

As David approached Alice, she brought her hands to her face and wept for a few moments longer. She had nothing to say. David gently pulled her up from the piano bench and walked her out of the building, momentarily placing an arm about her slender frame as would a father.

They walked home in silence. David hated with all his heart to take her back to the halfway house, especially after this most recent experience. The dark spirit of that place would chase away the feeling.

"Alice, you need to know something."

She waited quietly.

"There was not a soul in that room tonight that you didn't touch with your music. I can't begin to describe the spirit of what I felt in there."

She nodded weakly.

"You can't pluck healthy fruit from a diseased tree, Alice. What you did tonight could not have been possible if you had nothing inside to share."

Alice remained too lost in thoughts to respond with more than a nod.

"Please, Alice, understand this one thing if you understand nothing else. You are *not* empty. You have so much to give."

As Alice slowly ascended the steps back into the halfway house, he wondered if she yet believed him.

No beast is more savage than man when
possessed with power answerable to his rage.

—Plutarch

# Chapter 9

A little gift from my wife," David explained as he held forth a tray of lasagna. "She wouldn't take no for an answer. She wanted you to have a decent meal around here for once."

Alice smiled and accepted the dish. There was something definitely different about her, David noticed. Since yesterday's impromptu piano recital, her face had less worry creased into it. She smiled more often even if still not very much.

"Thank you, and please thank your wife. I'll leave it in the fridge for now. I don't usually eat dinner for another hour yet."

"Go right ahead."

Alice opened the barren refrigerator and placed the dish next to a bottle of ketchup and a few microwave dinners—the only other contents in the fridge.

"If it's okay with you," Alice suggested, "I'd rather go for another walk today. No more surprises, though!" She pointed an accusing finger.

David laughed. "No surprises."

The overcast day, while a bit gloomy, remained far superior to the sickly air of that building. They strolled to a nearby park where the walkways were regularly plowed, which wasn't as big a concern now that most of the snow had finally melted.

Though the air stayed brisk the advancing season had finally chased away its bite. Already the perennials poked bravely out of the ground to signal spring's arrival.

Alice tightened her coat to ward off the chill.

"There's something I've been wondering about," she said. "Don't be offended, but from what you've told me of your life so far, I don't understand how you didn't end up in a mental hospital or rehab center. Or dead, for that matter."

Echoes of the past surfaced in David's memory. Many others before Alice had wondered that very thing, some of them doctors.

"Many of my closest friends went that route," he said.

Alice walked in thoughtful silence for a moment. "But you seem so . . . normal. I can't understand how such an upbringing wouldn't ruin you."

"It did," David answered.

Alice stopped and looked quizzically at David. "I thought you told me that you were happy?"

"I am. I also said, on our first visit you may recall, that no matter how broken I was I could still be fixed. Make no mistake Alice, I truly *was* broken. Ruined. And I stayed that way for a long, long time."

She folded her hands behind her back, waiting for him to continue.

David couldn't believe his good luck. Dad had left Ina. Now he, Billy, and Dad lived in an apartment over a great pizza store and he hadn't seen Ina or Karl in over six months. Dad still made sure that they worked a lot, but nowhere near what they used to. It had taken awhile for things to settle down with the move and all, but they were finally done.

Up until his current age of fourteen, life had been one horrible experience after another. Now he could look forward to the fact that from here on out would be smooth sailing.

"Hey Billy, you goin' to the football game tonight?"

"No. I've got homework."

"Suit yourself," David answered. "I'll let you know how it goes."

Although David was only in junior high school, he loved attending the high school football games. Especially against their main rival, who they'd play in tonight's game. In these rival matches, the teams played their hardest and brought the biggest crowds. Great half-time shows, too.

David hopped on his bike and pedaled the short distance to the high school. He chained his bike to a telephone pole and bought a ticket in, and then scanned the crowd for some of his friends.

"Hey, David!" a voice called. "Over here."

He recognized the voice. His friend Tim. Ryan sat with him.

"Game's about to start," said Tim. "We saved you a seat." Tim's scrawny body ensured that plenty of people picked on him on a regular basis, but he was still pretty tough for his size. *One of these days,* David thought, *somebody will pick on Tim and get more than they bargained for.*

"Here, have some lemonade," Ryan said.

The referee blew the whistle. David sat down and rubbed his hands in anticipation and then began sipping his drink. This would be a great game.

The opposing team was first on defense. The kick went high and long, nearly to the end zone before one of the players from his home team caught the ball. From that moment on, the two teams were at war on the field.

David loved it. Play after play, each team fought harder than he would have believed possible, as though lives were at stake. When his home town scored a touchdown only two minutes into the first quarter, he thought that they had the game in the bag. Then the rivals scored a touchdown of their own on the very next play and David realized this would be an even better game than he'd hoped for. In his opinion the best games were the closest, no matter who won.

Neck and neck, the game inched on with the two teams so

evenly matched it seemed for sure they'd have to go into over-time.

At last the lemonade running through David's body demanded that he take a break shortly before half-time.

"Save my spot!" he yelled and then scrambled along the bench to the stairs between the isles. The crowd was already on their feet with excitement, so he didn't bother anybody by his standing up. After dodging some kids selling candy and hotdogs to raise money for new band instruments, he double-checked his pocket to make sure he hadn't left his ticket at his seat and ran over to the bathroom. He didn't want to miss any more of the game than he had to.

Not twenty steps away from the gate, he heard the sounds of painful crying. The cries turned his stomach and filled him with a sense of anxiety.

David followed the sounds of crying into the bathroom and then rushed inside to witness something that chilled his blood. There in the back corner of the bathroom two older kids from his home town were wailing on a younger kid from the rival town. The sight took David's breath away. Anger swelled within him at each passing second.

"Hey, want a couple of free hits on the sissy?" one of them called to David. "We'll hold him for you." The kid they were roughing up looked ready to fall over. They had not been merely teasing. He had a cut mouth and two black eyes. Soon those eyes would swell tremendously.

"Leave him alone," David threatened.

Their smiles slipped instantly. The two boys, each probably a year older than David, tightened their grip on the kid from the rival school and took a step forward.

"What'd you say to us?" the shorter one asked.

"I said leave him alone."

The second boy laughed. "That's it. You're dead meat."

From that moment on, instinct alone fueled his actions. Common sense and logic faded away as pure, unrestrained rage ripped control from his mind. David could only vaguely hear the cries of surprise and pain as he launched into the two boys, swinging and attacking in any way he could.

They might have fought back. He didn't notice. He only saw that they were trying to hurt an innocent person. Their cruelty triggered within David an avalanche of resentment and injustice that had formed year after merciless year. The two boys desperately trying to get away from him embodied all that he had been forced to go through. He could finally lash out. Finally attack back.

Everything became a blur.

When he ultimately regained his senses, David stood over the two boys cowering in the bathroom corner. Their screams of pain and pleading that he stop finally registered in his ears. The boy they had been beating up crouched in the opposite corner, wide-eyed.

David glanced down and saw his hands covered with blood.

Horrified, he looked at the two kids he had fought. With relief, he noticed that they only had bloodied noses and more than a few bumps and bruises. He hadn't done any serious damage.

Once they could see David would let them by, both boys scrambled out of the bathroom as fast as they could. David turned to the other kid while still trying to come back to his senses. He simply stared at the kid without speaking while his brain slowly returned to normal.

This was happening more and more. It seemed like fights kept finding him lately, no matter where he went. The moment somebody threatened him he went berserk.

And scariest of all, he could barely control himself while in that state or even remember details afterward. It terrified David to no end when he thought about what he might someday do to someone when he went crazy like that.

He took a step toward the other boy, who shrunk even more into the corner.

"Are you okay?" he asked the other boy.

The boy finally found courage enough to run out of the bathroom without a word.

Before leaving himself, David took a few minutes to try and cool down even more. He stared at his reflection in the mirror, surprised again at how much his face changed during times like this. The kid in the mirror looked terrifying. That wasn't him!

At last he calmed enough to where he could at least recognize his own face.

"That's better."

Leaving the bathroom, David's blood turned cold once again as he saw a small group glancing in his direction with obvious intentions. The boys he had just fought stood off a little distance with someone several years older than David. They were hiding behind this tower of muscle and pointing at David as he left the bathroom.

*Oh please,* David thought. *Not again. Not already. This isn't fair.*

The older brother, cousin, or whoever, pointed at David.

"You! Come here you little punk. You're gonna wish you never laid hands on my brother. I'm gonna stomp ya."

Blackout.

The next thing David remembered was Officer Brown's soothing voice.

"Calm down, David," the officer said in an even tone. "He's had enough."

But David couldn't understand what Officer Brown wanted or why he was even there. He only lived in the anger of the moment, lost in some powerful struggle inside that he could feel but not define.

Another voice rose to the surface of his foggy brain. A woman's voice, he thought.

"Aren't you going to stop it?" she asked. She sounded pretty upset.

"You stop it," Officer Brown answered. "I'm letting him finish."

*Finish? Finish what?* David wondered. *What do I need to finish?*

"David," Officer Brown said again. A trace of impatience laced his voice. "Now come on. That's enough. Take it easy."

Suddenly David realized he was kneeling on the ground. And not alone. He knelt on top of somebody.

And, his fists were clenched.

He came out of the fog even more and noticed for the first time the person beneath him. A man he didn't recognize was covering his face with both hands. The man's face and hands were covered in blood and bruises, with grass stains and long rips all throughout his shirt.

David turned around and saw people staring at him in disgust. He stood up, ashamed. Then he remembered. There had been a boy in the bathroom. A boy getting hurt. And then this man outside who threatened him . . .

That man now lay on the ground writhing in pain.

"Come on, David," Officer Brown said. "You and I need to have a talk."

Officer Brown grabbed David by the arm and led him away quickly. Officer Brown seemed awfully mad at the moment, which wasn't like him.

"Throw that freak in jail!" somebody called out. David never bothered to glance back. Shame overwhelmed him as he walked toward the police cruiser. Something was going terribly wrong with him. He had turned into some kind of monster back there. He couldn't even remember what had happened.

"Get in the car," Officer Brown said.

David climbed in the back seat, quiet. He liked Officer Brown. And now he had upset him. Guilt began to set in slow but sure.

Officer Brown climbed in and started the police car up. He pulled out without a word and drove down the street. Once they had traveled a half mile or so, Officer Brown turned around and grinned.

David blinked. He hadn't expected a grin.

"Boy, you're something else," Officer Brown said while turning another corner. This particular street would not take them to the police station. "Now I'm supposed to tell you what a horrible thing you've done tonight, but I don't think I can bring myself to."

"But that guy was in a lot of pain. I did that."

Officer Brown laughed. "David, that waste of life you were pounding into the grass has beat up more younger kids than I can keep track of. A couple girlfriends too. And his younger brother's following in the same footsteps. That's the first time I can think of that either of them got a taste of their own medicine."

Officer Brown turned up a side street toward the ice cream shop. "Truth is, you might've even saved some people from getting a licking in the future. I think that deserves a milk shake. Chocolate or vanilla?"

"Chocolate," David answered in a haze. His head still couldn't clear.

They drove around in the police car for another hour like they did most Friday nights. The cops in this town had taken an interest in him lately for some reason. As David sipped his milk shake, he tried to laugh at Officer Brown's jokes. He tried to feel good.

But he couldn't get that image of himself in the mirror out of his mind. Especially his own eyes. He counted it sheer dumb luck that the people he had been in fights with tonight had not suffered any broken bones or other serious damage. He also tried to tell himself that they had it coming, like Officer Brown said. They were bullies and he had only given them a sample of what they had put others through.

Yet he knew better than to pat himself on the back. He had a problem on his hands. A big problem. These guys tonight might have been bullies, but they could just as easily have been nice people in the wrong situation. Plus, he could have hurt them a lot worse than he did.

And all they had to do, David knew, was make the slightest threat against him or someone else and he turned into an animal. For that matter, even if somebody might say something innocent or as a joke and he thought it was real he'd react the same way. That single thought kept him from enjoying the milk shake or laughing at Officer Brown's stories. David couldn't trust himself any more.

He had no control over when that animal might come loose, or what it might do.

The possibilities scared him more than he wanted to admit.

For the next several weeks David avoided any football games. He avoided people whenever he could. Even though he wanted to feel happy and relax with his friends, he remained worried about what might happen if they got to playing rough and he lost control again.

This wasn't supposed to happen, he told himself. He and Billy were living alone with Dad and their lives finally headed in the right direction.

And then something wonderful began to happen. As the weeks turned to months, his patience paid off. From avoiding confrontation and sports at all costs he realized that he could stay away from turning into that monster in the mirror. He began to forget all about the incident at the football game. It had been nothing more than a really bad day after all. A leftover from the dark days of his early childhood. Something that he wouldn't repeat.

He started playing with friends again, even a little bit of wrestling around with them, and finally started to see the rainbow ahead of him bright and clear once more. The worst had passed.

And then he and Billy came home from school one afternoon, opened the door to the living room, and saw Ina snuggling on the couch with Dad as though nothing had ever happened.

David fought back the blackout.

Beware when reason can no longer be heard above the storm within.

—Michael W. Rickson

# Chapter 10

Three months had passed since Ina moved back in and already David's life had fallen to pieces once again. He stood with clenched fists while she yelled at him. Billy stood off in the corner, silent as always.

"You're just as lazy as when I left ya!" she screamed. "Didn't ya learn nothing from me? In one little year your dad done ruined ya. Now you wash those plates spotless, or you can go outside and get a willow!"

All his life he had done what she told him. Then Dad left her and for one whole year they had lived without her around. In that time, David had tasted freedom for the first time. And all at once his freedom had disappeared as quickly as it had arrived. For the past three months, some of the hardest in his life, he had followed her demands without question. A lifetime of fear in her presence made him do so, but he couldn't do it today.

Not today, or ever again. If he didn't take a stand, she would rule his life forever.

"No," he said. "You get up off your lazy butt and do it yourself!"

Ina glared at him with a mixture of shock and pure contempt. Billy looked up, equally stunned that David had stood up to her.

Ina took a deep breath. "You better take back them words,

son, or you'll get the whippin' of a lifetime."

But David was beyond caring about her threats. The very animal she had reduced him to began to surface. "I said no. No more. You don't tell me what to do ever again. And if you lay a hand on me, you better be prepared for what happens after that."

Ina didn't hesitate. She lunged forward and slapped David full in the face. The moment she did so, however, she realized her mistake. Ina scrambled backward in a rush as David swung a closed fist at her and barely missed.

"Get back from me, you devil!" she screamed.

She positioned herself on the other side of the table, temporarily out of his reach. David was prepared to smash the table to pieces in an effort to reach her until he saw an easier solution.

Years of pain and anxiety boiled to a head as he grabbed a large can of soup from the pantry. He clutched the can tightly for a moment while staring at her. Ina was a black cloud of misery floating around at will and poisoning everybody she came across. His resentment for her seemed to magnify by the second. This woman would not go away. Why wouldn't she?! He didn't want her there.

She watched him warily.

Before Ina could so much as make another sound, David hurled the can of soup directly at her face. He watched with satisfaction as it rocketed through the air, aiming dead-on for her forehead. He couldn't wait to watch it hit.

Almost as if in slow-motion, he saw Billy's hand shoot out from nowhere and collide with the can of soup, knocking it out of the air.

"What'd you do that for?" David screamed. He couldn't believe that the can hadn't hit her. Billy cheated him out of it. Her face had gone pale with fright, but he wanted to see it shrieking in pain. After all she had done to them, he needed to see her destroyed. He had to unleash all the pent-up anger, and Billy had stopped it from happening.

David made another lunge at her across the table, but Billy

grabbed him by the arm and yanked him back. Though Billy was far stronger, David fought with everything he had to reach Ina, who by then had crouched defensively in a corner. The world around David blurred so thoroughly he could see nothing but the object of his hatred standing in front of him. No sooner could he have understood what Billy yelled in his ear than he could have willed his heart to stop beating. Bit by bit, Billy managed to drag David out the front door and onto the second-story stairwell.

Once outside, David noticed his brother's bloodied hand for the first time.

"What happened to your hand?" David asked, angry all over again. Ina must have done it. Cut him with a knife or something. He tried to make another dash inside the building when Billy crushed him in a bear hug.

"Get in the car David," Billy said. His intensity finally snapped David back to reality enough to listen. He allowed his brother to half-walk, half-shove him down the stairs and into their shared car. Billy hopped in the driver's seat and took off as quickly as the car would allow.

They rode in silence for a bit. David still wondered where all that blood on his brother's hand came from. What had Ina done? He would make her pay for it. For that, and everything else. She would pay.

"You coulda killed her with that can," Billy said at last.

For a few moments David forced his mind to focus. He tried to remember what Billy was talking about.

"What can?"

Billy shook his head. "The one you threw at Ina's head hard enough to split her skull open. *That* can."

Clarity came back in a rush. The can of soup. And Billy had batted it out of the air. Billy's hand. Guilt tumbled in by the truckload as he realized he had been the one who hurt Billy.

"Billy . . . I'm so sorry, is your hand okay?"

Billy laughed as he tore off a strip of shirt and wrapped it around his bleeding hand. "This is nothing. But you need to calm down around her, David. I don't like her being here any more than you do, but do you want to end up in jail?"

"No, it's only that—"

"You can't help it. I know. But David, you better learn how or you're gonna do something you'll regret. I won't always be there to stop you."

David said nothing. As horrible as it sounded, he couldn't decide for sure if he was glad Billy had stopped him. Even now with his head a bit clearer he wondered if the world would be better off if Billy had let that can hit her. It probably wouldn't have killed her. Just shattered her nose or something. Then maybe she would leave for good.

"But man," Billy said, laughing, "I don't think I'll ever forget that look on her face when you finally told her off. I've dreamt about that for years."

David didn't join in on the joke. His mind still churned with all the turmoil Ina stirred up. As great as the year with Dad had been, she had already more than ruined whatever happiness they had enjoyed simply by her being there. He couldn't think of anything as much as his desire to be away from Ina.

They drove for an hour or two, trying to forget the experience. They spoke about some good times that they'd had, girls they liked, and about some plans they wanted to make for next summer. Anything but Ina. Part of the bond of their brotherhood lay in the unspoken understanding about what they could and could not talk about, and when. Right now, any further mention of Ina would've sent David off the deep end again and Billy knew that. The whole point of the drive was to calm down.

At the end of the drive, Billy parked the car by the stairs to their little apartment over the pizza store. David sat still for a moment, gathering the courage to walk in there again. If only Dad stuck around more often. He'd been gone over a month now.

He shook the fact of Dad's absence from his mind. It's not like that would change any time soon. The immediate problem was Ina. He had to face her all over again. He took comfort in the fact that he had shaken her up a bit. Maybe she would mind her own business from here on out.

Yeah, right. And maybe Dad would stop drinking.

"You ready?" Billy asked.

"I guess so," David said. "If one of us is stayin' out of our apartment it's her. Not me."

"David," Billy warned.

"I know, I know. Stay calm. I will."

They walked up the stairs and David heard Ina yelling. Ina certainly screamed often enough, but she didn't have any friends nearby. He wondered who she could be giving an earful to right now. Possibly the landlord coming to collect rent. In her mood she'd probably yell at about anyone who crossed her path.

When he opened the door, however, he saw Dad standing in front of her, looking pretty upset. She whipped around like a snake when the door opened and pointed an accusing finger at David.

"There he is!" she screamed. "Your little freak of a son that tried to kill me! And for nothing!"

"David," Dad said sternly, "what in the hell has gotten into you?"

All at once, David's defenses vanished. Any restraint he might have exercised in the past was no longer his to draw upon. The fragile remnants of support beams to his self control were kicked away.

Through the lens of his rage, he saw in Ina a twisted woman, a filthy person full of hate. A woman trying to turn his dad against him. She had been the source of so much pain. Everything came rushing in at once. The merciless beatings, the slave work. Her stealing their money. Ina's constant criticism. All the nights that David lay awake in pain, wondering if she would beat him to death. The fear and loathing of this woman.

It all boiled up into a dark storm cloud crackling with enough electricity to level a town. The enormous energy worked its way through his body, narrowing his vision and surging his muscles with power and need.

The only thing in the world at that moment was the threat in front of him. A singular threat that had ruined so much of his life and one which was positioned to ruin the rest of it as well. David knew for the first time in his life the only true way to end this threat.

Kill it.

He dove at her with a scream and locked his hands around her neck in a death grip. He crushed her throat with every ounce of strength he possessed. The serpent beneath his hands began thrashing, but soon buckled under his strength. She could not stand. He smiled. It was working. She couldn't fight back. She would die in a few short glorious minutes and he'd be free. Finally free . . .

A force of strength that dwarfed his own ripped him off before he could finish crushing the life out of his enemy. He kicked and fought to end the poison that was Ina. He had to kill the poison or it would come back. It always did. But his thrashing could not prevail against the arms of iron that wrenched him away from her. Safely away from him, she coughed and hacked through tears, still alive. Still alive!

She should be dead, but he remained powerless to finish the act of making it happen.

David wanted to cry.

How much time passed before David could come back to any semblance of normality he had no way of knowing. When he finally grew aware enough of his surroundings to recognize his own family, he noticed Ina fuming over in the corner, shrieking words he couldn't hear. Dad stood in front of him appearing now not so much angry as confused.

"Billy, what's the matter with your brother?" he asked. "David's not . . . crazy, is he?"

Ina screamed her opinion as to the answer for that question but Billy was still too worked up emotionally to respond right away.

"No, Dad," David said quickly. "I'm not crazy." He glared at Ina. "But I want her out of our lives. Forever."

"What's wrong with Ina?" Dad asked.

Dad had been gone most of the time during their early years.

This was something that had caused David and Billy both a lot of pain. They loved him, and they knew that he loved them. He always watched out for them when he could. But he never knew, not even a little, what had been going on. She had them terrified too far to speak out against her. Even a year ago with Karl, they hadn't told a tenth of what Ina had done to them.

That was all about to change.

"Dad," David said, forcing his voice to stay calm, "there are some things about her you need to know once and for all."

Dad listened first with disbelief, then with shock, then with anger as David summarized their life under her care. Billy found his voice too and unloaded everything she had done to them. For once, Ina stayed completely silent when Dad glared at her. She had the fear of death written all over her face.

For the better part of an hour he and Billy hit the highlights, or low points rather, of what Ina had inflicted upon them during the years. Everything from the bullwhip to stealing their lunch money. Dad became visibly sick as the details surfaced.

At one point, Dad demanded an answer from Ina over something especially horrible and, rather than answer, she tried running out of the room. Dad's anger had grown so fast and powerful in the previous hour that he ran after her and snatched her by the back of the hair. With one powerful motion and by gripping nothing but that handful of hair he yanked her clear off the floor and out of the doorway she tried fleeing through.

It left a bald spot on the back of her head the size of a grapefruit, something that made David laugh, even though it shouldn't have been funny. Ina screamed at the pain but knew better than to try and strike back.

As Dad and Ina continued to yell and argue, David wondered if they would get back together after this. If they did, now at least Dad knew once and for all what kind of a woman he had married all those years ago. A huge sense of relief washed over him at having finally unloaded all those secrets. Even so, if David knew Ina like he did, she'd find a way to weasel her way back into Dad's life sooner or later.

As he watched Dad and Ina scream at each other, David decided that whether they patched things up or not didn't concern him anymore. If he ever saw this woman again, there was no telling what he'd do to her. He didn't want to go to jail on her account, nor did he want to suffer another minute in her presence. A single solution presented itself that struck him as so simple and effective he couldn't believe he hadn't thought of it years earlier.

He would move away from home.

David's friend Marcus raised a bottle of beer in a toast. "This is the life, ain't it boys?"

David and Chad joined the toast with bottles of their own. They drank the night away in the old cabin that had become their own. Marcus's older brother had bought them the beer, and David had found the abandoned cabin they were staying in. No heating, no electricity, no plumbing, but better than any place he'd ever lived.

After living so long under Ina's thumb, David couldn't believe how good freedom felt. He'd moved out from home that same day he and Ina had the big fight. For a couple months he kept trying to go to school until he showed up late for class one day. A couple friends had wrestled him down in the hallway to make him late, just for fun. Not that he minded or anything. He'd been late plenty of times before.

But when he walked late into class that particular day the teacher said in front of the class, 'You know Dave, you're a worthless piece of garbage. Why don't you just do us all a favor and leave?' That very day he quit school and he hadn't so much as given it a second thought these past few months.

In any case he didn't need school. He had his own place. True, the abandoned cabin didn't have much, but that didn't matter so much in the summer time. Marcus had said it right. This *was* the life.

These were the same hills that Ina had made him and Billy go hike to for work back in his early childhood. How different the hills felt now with her out of the picture. David wondered what Billy was up to. He hadn't seen him in a couple months. Still, he didn't worry. Anything would be better than living with Ina. Even the gutter. Billy would be fine.

"Hey, pass me another one," David said. Chad tossed a beer over the rickety table they had built from scrap wood.

David took another swig from the bottle. When he had first tasted beer not all that long ago he couldn't understand why his dad liked drinking it so much. He had almost thrown up. But, after a couple of times the taste began to grow on him. And he loved getting drunk, even though the hangovers afterward took away some of the thrill.

When he was drunk he didn't have a care in the world. He liked that most of all. David knew he would never drink as heavy as Dad or anything, but he liked when he could occasionally come across beer of one kind or another. At fifteen, getting his hands on stuff to drink didn't take nearly as much effort as he'd thought it would. And way out here in the middle of nowhere they would never get caught no matter what they drank.

"Hey, is Kris coming out to see you today?" Chad asked.

David winked. "Yeah. Wonder if she'll bring me any food?" The others laughed at the sarcasm. Of course she would. For reasons David couldn't guess at, lots of girls—especially Kris—tried to take care of him out in this little shack of a building. They all thought he would starve to death otherwise or something. He hadn't gone hungry more than a meal or two, and he didn't have a dime to spend on food. He could definitely get used to not working. He figured this was his time to make up for all the years he stayed on his feet for eighteen hours at a stretch.

A knock sounded on the door and a young girl poked her head in the room.

"Kris!" David called out. "Come on in."

+ + +

"I'm telling you, I'm not going home," David said, tacking up another blanket over the windows. "You guys leave if you want but I'm staying here."

The summer had flown by way too fast. He didn't want it to end already, but the cabin would soon grow too cold to sleep in. If he sealed off enough of the drafts, though, he thought he could make the place warm and dry enough to live in anyway. He'd have to find a way to bring some firewood out here, but he'd rather risk freezing to death than move back home.

The parties, drinking, and girls spoiling him aside, what he truly couldn't leave behind was the freedom. He'd sooner face a winter in this shack without so much as a stick of firewood than go and live with Ina again.

"But you'll get sick," Marcus said. "You might even die. You can't sleep when it gets below zero. Not in a place like this!"

"I'll figure out a way," David said. "I ain't going back and that's it."

Chad brightened all of a sudden. "Hey, I got it! Come and stay with me for the winter!"

David laughed. "Oh, ha, ha. Very funny. Now hand me another blanket."

"No, I'm serious. My parents are gone all the time anyway. We've got the extra bed since my older brother moved out. They'd let you stay. I know they would."

David cocked his head to the side. That sounded like far too easy a solution to actually work. Especially for him. "I don't think they'd go for it, man. They don't even know me."

"At least let me ask them, then?"

"Okay," David said. "*If* they say yes, of course I'd stay with you during the winter. But if not, I'm taking my chances out here."

Chad clapped his hands together. "Yeah! This is gonna be awesome."

Marcus smiled too. "We gotta stick together, right?" Marcus lived only a block away from Chad.

Even while laughing along with his friends, David knew that

it was pointless to get their hopes up. Chad's parents would say no. Easy breaks simply didn't come to him.

David couldn't believe his luck. Chad's parents hadn't even needed time to think over whether he could stay there during the winter. No problem at all, they'd said. And he could stay free of charge. For the first time in his life, something fantastic had dropped right in his lap, and he didn't even have to fix things up like he did with the shack. Why, oh why, hadn't he left home sooner?

As Chad said, his parents were gone a lot of the time. At bars, mostly. Nothing new to David. Still, they hit the bars even more than Dad or Ina. He had thought Dad was a pretty big drinker, but he didn't even come close compared to these people.

In addition to hitting the bars, they filled their refrigerator with all kinds of beer, vodka, whisky—you name it. Once in a while, he and Chad would sample some of the open bottles from the refrigerator when nobody was around. They were careful not to drink so much that somebody might notice.

After sampling several drinks, he found that he liked the strong taste of vodka more than about anything else. Those first couple samples were a little more intense than he'd expected but he quickly came to enjoy the strength of it. Chad's family always kept plenty of vodka on hand too, so he and Chad could usually sneak it pretty easy.

One morning, David tiptoed over to the refrigerator before the house woke up. It was pretty early in the morning, only a little bit after dawn, and he couldn't sleep. He thought he'd take a tiny little swig of his favorite drink before Chad's folks got up and left the house.

He heard footsteps round the corner right as he lifted the bottle to his lips. He froze as Chad's father stared down at him, a fifteen-year-old, swiping vodka. David cursed his own stupidity. Why hadn't he at least had the good sense to wait until they had gone? Now he'd cost himself a home for the winter. Stupid. Stupid, stupid, *stupid.*

But the man only stood there and cracked a smile. "Starting a little young, ain't ya?"

David couldn't think of what to say.

"Here, join me for breakfast since you're up." Chad's father placed two large glasses down on the table and jerked the bottle away from David.

He poured generously from the bottle into each glass. Taking one for himself, he held the other out for David.

David knew the man was joking. He had to be. But no, he continued to offer the cup, waiting for David to take it.

"You're gonna do it anyway; there's no sense in tryin' to stop you. Besides, it clears a man's head. Drink up."

Finally, David accepted the drink and held it to his lips. Before he had only ever had small sips, just enough to get the taste in his mouth. Not a complete drink like this.

He took a long swallow and felt his throat burn. The man laughed as David made a face, but David wouldn't look the fool in front of his friend's father no matter how much it hurt. He took another long swallow, and then another, barely flinching.

Though the fiery liquid burned his throat, it excited David. He set down the empty cup and stared right back at the man.

"That's good, I like a man who can drink like one." Chad's father swallowed his without effort and set the empty cup down beside David's. He reached and patted David on the back.

"Same time tomorrow, then," he said while leaving.

Only after Chad's father left the house would David allow himself to cough. While he did enjoy the exciting burn of the vodka, he still couldn't help but feel like he'd just swallowed a couple of hot coals from a fire pit. His throat continued to throb, but in a good way. A strong way.

Besides, soon enough he'd be able to drink it and hardly feel the burn. The way Chad's father could. The way his own father could.

A manly way, as he liked to think of it.

No one can wear a mask for very long.

—Seneca

# Chapter 11

Music blasted in the background. David jumped up on the table, to the laughter and approval of everyone there. It was his time in the spotlight. Nobody could keep up with David when he got like this.

"Time for dancing!" David shouted. He took a long swig of beer and started doing some nonsense dance on top of the table. Young girls laughed, and he pulled a couple of them up to join in with him.

The wood groaned beneath their combined weight. David began unbuttoning his shirt to the music, teasing the girls in the room. They brought out dollar bills and whistled between their teeth.

David ate it up. He was born to be the life of the party.

Somebody tossed up a cowboy hat and David snatched it out of the air. His dance transformed into a mock rodeo, bull-riding style. The girls up with him shrieked with laughter and then jumped back down as David rocked and stomped on the tabletop.

With a loud crack, the table broke clean in two and sent David flying into the wall.

He hit it hard, but leaped right back on his feet. "Did I last eight seconds?"

The other kids at the party laughed hysterically at David's

quick wit. All but the kid whose house they partied at, of course. He stared horrified at his parent's now-broken table.

David walked over to the poor guy and put an arm around his shoulder. Jason, he thought his name was.

"It coulda been worse," David said. "At least it had a quick death. The table didn't suffer."

More laughter. Jason managed a weak smile.

Three of the girls sauntered up to David, winking.

"Pretty impressive, stud," one of them said. "What else can you do?"

Laughing, David decided he could step aside from the lime-light long enough to follow this new development.

By three in the morning, David gave up trying to fall to sleep. Once the house had fallen silent, but for the snoring of his friends, anxiety had begun crushing him with its vicious tenacity, scarcely letting him breath. It had grown steadily worse for the last hour and a half.

He slipped out of his bed and walked into the living room. Old pizza boxes and beer bottles littered the floor. David pulled out an old wooden chair and sat down in it, facing backward. By now his hyperventilating had reached the point where he suspected he might pass out.

As he always did in times like this, he slouched down and placed his forehead against the top of the chair back, then used his arms to block out the remaining visibility. His world, or at least all of it that he could see, shrank to only the few inches between his face and the back of the chair. Through the slits in the chair back he could glimpse other parts of the trash-filled room, but sitting like this he could block those other images out.

His breathing didn't slow. A sense of foreboding, an awful dread for the empty time stretching out in front of him, continued to course through his body. These attacks effectively crippled him until they passed. Weekends were always the worst. If he could go to work, that would distract him. He worked as long as he possibly could, as hard as he could, for fear that the anxiety and pain would start to creep in otherwise.

Despite his efforts to calm down, David's muscles tightened cruelly. He thought he heard his back cracking again.

The parties helped, sometimes, but only for a little while. Earlier this evening he had met those three girls—their names had already slipped his mind—and he'd had some fun with their company.

But, as always, once the party ended and the alcohol buzz wore off he had started sweating in nervousness.

If he could only find enough ways to stay busy. If only he didn't have to sleep. Or sometimes he wondered if it would be better to hardly ever wake up. To always sleep. He would gladly choose the worst nightmare over this feeling of helplessness. But that horrible window between waking and sleeping became a daily battle for him where his problems could rise up and dance in the shadows of his skull, tormenting him. Weekends especially.

David gripped the chair slats tight enough to cause the wooden joints to squeak in protest. His whole body began to shake. Anxiety overwhelmed him. Life consisted of pain and anguish—all else was temporary. He had nothing to live for and everything to fear.

Why did life have to be like this? David wanted to scream to the heavens. What was wrong with him? No matter how hard he tried to stay safe from his own demons, they continually swarmed him in the quiet and lonely moments. Even if he did nothing but sit still, eventually his own special hell oozed to the surface as sure as the sun would rise the next day.

Except that in the grip of these attacks, he felt certain that the sun would never rise again. Give him an enemy to fight, and he would unleash this pain in a moment. Give him a threat to strike at, and he would not hesitate. But he had no way to attack the silence. Nor to fight the fears that seemingly sought to kill him.

His breathing grew even more rapid. David began to feel light-headed. He didn't fight it this time. Let it come, he figured. Let him pass out. It would end things if only for a brief while.

He tried breathing faster to aid in losing consciousness but the sharpness of the pain inside kept him alert. The anxiety—pure and naked fear of nothing and everything—wouldn't even let him give way to passing out.

In a fit of desperate frustration, David jumped up and hurled the chair into the brick fireplace. He tasted a moment's satisfaction as the chair splintered against the unyielding brick, but it faded all too quickly.

Hurried footsteps came into the room.

"What the hell's goin' on?" Mark asked. Mark held a baseball bat, searching around the room for an intruder.

David stood alone, his chest rising and falling with the effort to try and push back the anxiety attack. Shattering the chair had done nothing to turn back the tide. He felt as though he were about to rip apart from the inside out. He wanted to lunge at Mark, just to have something to aim his suffering at. Anything to unleash it.

But he restrained. Mark might have been a bit on the selfish side, but David still counted him as a friend. If nothing else, he hadn't done anything bad to David.

Mark finally noticed the shattered chair. Several bricks had been cracked from the impact, and at least one had been knocked loose. The crumbled remains of brick and chair lay in a heap on the floor.

"Did you do that? Man, what's wrong with you? Breaking Jason's table wasn't enough for one night?" Mark lowered the bat but didn't seem any less angry. "My parents are coming home in three days. You gonna buy a new chair before then?"

In his current state, David could barely hear Mark, but he knew enough to realize that he had better get out of there as soon as possible or he would lose control over what happened next. He walked to the refrigerator and grabbed his car keys from the rusted magnetic peg, ignoring Mark's questioning. By then Tim and Nathan had stumbled into the front room as well, though they stayed quiet while Mark screamed at David.

"What, are you so drunk you can't talk?" Mark yelled. "I said are you gonna pay for that chair? And what about the fireplace? What the hell's the matter with you anyway?"

Pushing back the urge to take a swing at Mark, David headed for the front door. He needed to leave before anything happened that he'd regret. Mark had no idea what kind of a person David could become. They had only known each other for a few weeks.

Tim, however, knew David quite well.

"Mark, shut up right now," Tim said. "Trust me on this one. I ain't kiddin'."

"What are you takin' his side for? You're crazy if you think—"

"Worry about it later, man. I'm serious. Just shut up. Now."

As Tim tried to talk Mark down, David continued toward the front door. Not about to give in so quickly, Mark took three quick steps and intercepted him. He stood there with his bat held high again in challenge.

"I ain't shutting up until he answers me." He glared at David. "I said are you gonna pay for that?"

With all his heart David wanted to wrench that bat out of Mark's hands and pound him right through the floor. He knew that ultimately Mark didn't deserve it, but he also knew that if Mark made so much as one threat with that bat, he would lose control.

On impulse, he stormed into the bathroom to try and cool off, shutting and locking the door behind him. The doorknob jiggled as somebody tried it from the other end. He heard the sounds of a brief scuffle behind the door, and some yelling, but didn't pay any attention.

The anxiety attack had already started making his hands shake. He flipped on the light and caught sight of himself in the medicine cabinet mirror. He hated seeing the animal inside staring back at him so boldly in the reflection. In a moment of rage he lunged forward and ripped the entire medicine cabinet off the wall. He turned and hurled it against the bathtub, shattering both cabinet and plaster alike.

Someone began banging on the bathroom door.

David screamed, long and loud, and rushed over to the shower. He kicked hard at the damaged area in the tub. Relief washed over him as he finally found something he could pit his pain against. His muscles bulged with the effort as he kicked at the shattering bath tub.

The plaster might as well have been straw. David's foot crashed through it with little if any resistance. The sweet destruction invigorated him. David viewed with enormous satisfaction the gaping hole where he had kicked. In his delirious state, he could imagine this room as representing the pain inside of him.

Plaster dust mingled with the broken glass from the mirror in the base of the tub.

He picked up the metal cabinet and began using it as a sledge-hammer. David took another swing at the tub. Then another. Then he attacked the tiles in the shower above, causing them to cascade down in shattered fragments. It might have been only painted plaster and tile giving way before him, but David noticed a measure of his pain disappear with them. He swung again, chasing after a release from the anxiety.

After demolishing the shower he stepped out of the rubble and kicked over the toilet. Water splashed everywhere. With his cabinet mallet he crushed the porcelain structure to tiny pieces, wrecking it as he shrieked his hatred at the place.

Everything unbroken in the room, from the sink to the drawers beneath it, called out and mocked him. He destroyed the sink completely then removed the drawers and threw them, contents and all, into the walls, ravaging the sheetrock. His muscles burned from the effort, and the building groaned at the onslaught, but it was helping. Nothing else mattered.

Before long, David had reduced the entire room to a heap of broken glass, wood, and plaster. His energy far outlasted the destruction and so he wrenched free a wooden towel rod and started ripping even larger gashes in the sheetrock walls, ruining the place as thoroughly as would the worst tornado.

Pure pain transferred from him in a torrent and into the chaos he attacked. He very nearly blacked out in the process but this time his pain kept him coherent at least a little.

Nothing but the timbers beneath the sheetrock remained and the towel rod did no good against those. In response he started to pull at them with his own hands, kicking now and again to try and inflict more punishment on them.

Several of the two-by-fours snapped before he had finally vented enough anger to drop on his knees and stop. David looked down and noticed in surprise that his hands were covered in blood. Only then did he remember the stinging sensation from gripping the metal cabinet with the broken glass at its edges. Besides that, there had been some nails on the timbers in the walls that he had certainly scraped up against.

As the pain began to register fully in his hands, David's breathing slowed. While he never actually sought out physical pain, he could not deny the grounding effect it had on him. It gave him something to focus on. The physical pain, more so perhaps than the act of demolishing the room, gradually calmed him down.

He didn't bother to wrap his hands, or even to try and soothe the pain. He merely welcomed the constant throbbing while he knelt there, trying to regain composure. While letting his heart rate slow down, he began to grow aware of the sound of running water. Examining the room, he noticed the water pipe that had fed the toilet was cracked and leaking at an alarming rate. A half inch of water already covered the floor.

All at once the realization of what he'd done sank in. Anger vanished like water on a hot frying pan as remorse filled its place. This wasn't even his own house. It belonged to a friend. *What was his name?* Mark.

David opened the door and stepped out. A half dozen boys his own age—everybody who'd decided to stay the night from the party—hung back at a cautious distance. Mark stood in the middle of them with his baseball bat gripped, though not in anger. Deathly fear lay written all over his face.

"Mark . . . I'm so sorry," David began, but didn't bother finishing. He had already seen the look on Mark's face, along with everyone else in the house. Terror. Fear. Repulsion.

Even Tim, who knew David better, looked shocked and saddened.

Guilt spread through him like a thick poison and David choked on whatever words he might have thought to say. He remembered seeing that creature in the mirror before he ripped the cabinet off the wall. No wonder these people had been afraid.

Running out of the house with no one to stop him this time, David hopped in his '53 Chevy and fired up the engine. He exploded out of the driveway with a screech of tires.

The pounding in his head wouldn't go away. None of the pleasant imageries from the party earlier that night remained. He saw in his mind only the animal in the mirror and the reaction of his friends when that animal came out of its hiding place. How many of them would still consider him a friend after tonight?

As he drove down the street he continually obeyed one constant and passionate need: he had to find a way to escape this emotional pain and guilt. Maybe if he drove fast enough he would be able to leave it behind.

The speedometer crept toward ninety miles per hour.

A turn in the road rose up before him. Every instinct in his body told him that he would need to slow down for such an abrupt turn. But David dismissed the warnings. It didn't matter if the car flipped. He decided to hit the gas instead.

All four tires screeched in protest as David wrenched the wheel to the right. The car tipped up on its side several feet and David waited without emotion for the vehicle to flip. At least it would end the torment. He had nothing to fear. Nothing to live for.

But the car impossibly landed back on the road again. The tires found their grip and David drove straight once more. The cuts in his hand stung as he cranked the wheel hard to straighten out the car. No sense of relief greeted him at having not flipped over. In fact, the pain and rage doubled inside.

He shouted. Shouted at the top of his lungs to try and expel this hateful energy. Guilt had replaced anger, but that was a fire that burned with no less heat. Pounding his fists into the steering wheel, he continued screaming until he had no remaining breath. His throat hurt from the effort. David welcomed the pain.

Another turn. This one even sharper. He didn't slow down, and the car lifted much higher off the ground than before. This was it, he thought. Time to die. Momentum wouldn't allow it otherwise. He prepared for the jolt, the crash of metal, the shattering glass, the cloud of red. The tires could never endure such a turn.

But they did. As though shoved downward by some unseen hand, the car righted itself once more. The whole frame shook and trembled with the impact. David screamed again, this time in defiance of whatever god or demon had intervened.

Filled with a mixture of relief and resentment, David slammed on the breaks. The tires peeled and smoked beneath the demand and the car fishtailed on the road but at last came to a standstill.

"What do you want from me?!" he screamed into the night.

Then, covering his face with bloodied hands and shaking with exhaustion, he wept.

He who fights with monsters might take care lest he
thereby become a monster. And if you gaze for long
into an abyss, the abyss gazes also into you.

—Friedrich Nietzsche

# Chapter 12

"Those were dark days, Alice. Dark days." David exhaled and noticed that his breath misted in front of him. The evening, apparently not caring that the calendar said it was spring, had turned cold quickly.

Alice remained silent.

"While I never considered putting a gun to my head or jumping off a building, I was still for all intents and purposes suicidal. When I hit those turns going ninety miles an hour, I honestly didn't care if the car flipped or not. Life had crumbled into a pretty meaningless existence. Death didn't scare me a bit."

She didn't say anything; however, David knew that he had her interest. Obviously Alice had arrived at a similar point in her life. She didn't fear anything because she had decided that she had nothing to lose.

Finally Alice sat up straight and cleared her throat. "And . . . yet you still found some way through this. That's almost too hard to believe."

"Well, it didn't happen overnight, for one thing. It took many years before I could come to grips with a lot of this. You see, when I left home, I thought myself rid of Ina and my past, but it stuck with me. At age eighteen, when I married my first wife, for example, I was still a wreck."

"Oh?"

"Yes, it didn't start out on a very good note either. I drank enough vodka on the morning of my wedding day that I passed out right in the middle of the ceremony."

"Ouch," Alice said. "So then what? Were you happy being married?"

"Some of the time, yes. Especially when we had kids. Brinna, my daughter, and my son Eric brought me great happiness, although being married and even having children couldn't kill the anxiety and stress. I still drank a lot, went to parties, and lived the wild life. This great hole in me might as well have been a roaring furnace. No matter what I threw at it the emptiness only spread. Partying, work, alcohol, and even marriage couldn't fill that void."

He took a deep breath. "And I was still very volatile. The slightest provocation could turn disastrous."

David sat in the bar. Work had been a killer that day, and he needed to unwind. Kris and the kids would be fine until he got home. After four years of marriage, he had learned that if he didn't clear his head a bit first, he and Kris would probably end up arguing anyway. She'd understand why he needed to stick around a tad longer.

"Give me another one!" he yelled to Cheston. Cheston poured David's favorite draft, keeping the head on the beer in exactly the right way, and slid it down the counter.

Jack Strenton slid next to David and patted him on the shoulder. "Hey, David, what's this I hear about Mike wanting to trade cars back?"

David laughed. "He's just an idiot. He doesn't want to trade back; he wants both cars for himself, without paying me a dime."

Jack scrunched his eyes up in disbelief. "You're kiddin'?"

"Nope. When we traded those two cars last year, he intentionally kept the title. I didn't think nothing of it at the time, but now he says that because he has the title it's still his car. He wants it back. And since I gave him my title, he says that's his car too."

"You're not gonna give it to him!" Jack said.

"Of course not. That jackass can moan all he wants. He's even dumber than I thought if he believes he can actually pull it off. No court would give it to him and I'm not about to either."

Jack nodded. "That's damn right. We'll testify that you two traded fair and square. Half the town knows it. Ol' Mike would probably cheat his own mother if he thought he could get away with it."

They shared a few more rounds of beers, though David's mind didn't clear like he hoped it would. Mike demanding again yesterday that David give the car back had worked him up pretty good. He took his frustrations out at work today and wore out his muscles from the effort.

*What a complete ass,* David thought as he pictured Mike bringing up the missing title. As if that would make it legally his! What a total waste of skin Mike had turned out to be. The fact that he'd planned this all out a year ago bothered David most of all. Knowing that Mike had been waiting all that time with this stupid plan made David's blood boil.

*Enough worrying about it,* David decided. No way could Mike get the car from him and that was the end of it. He could choke on that title for all he cared.

Only an hour or two had passed before David decided to head home. Normally he'd stay longer, but he needed rest after working his body to exhaustion all day long. He wanted sleep and nothing else.

The drive home started to relax him a little until he crested a small hill and saw his old car parked by the potato warehouse. As soon as David came anywhere near, the driver pulled forward, blocking the road. Mike leaned out of the window and waved David into the parking lot. He and another person sat waiting in the car.

A definite warning flag ignited within David. He didn't rec-ognize the big man sitting in the passenger seat. Mike wouldn't stop hounding David about the car, he knew. He figured the time had come to tell Mike once and for all that he would never, ever get his car back. No way legally or otherwise.

Ignoring a rising sense of unease, David followed them into the parking lot.

Mike and his passenger threw the car into park. Mike, behind the wheel, opened the door without getting out of the car. David could now see the big guy in the other seat. At least 250 pounds, the guy was practically solid muscle.

An ugly expression appeared on Mike's face. "Now listen, David, that's my car." He held up a pink piece of paper. "This is the title that says so. If you don't give it to me right here and now, my friend is gonna beat you senseless."

All intentions to talk through the problem vanished.

The animal that resided always a breath away from the surface exploded into action. Years of survival created an instinct in David's hard-wiring that responded without conscious decision to do so. Punish or be punished.

Before the big man could even get out of the car, David had already covered the distance between himself and the driver's side door where Mike sat trembling. Rage ignited in David's psyche as quickly as a match tossed into a pool of gasoline.

With a face full of terror, Mike slammed the door shut before David could arrive. He obviously hadn't expected this.

The big man sat hesitant, watching.

When David reached the car, he yanked on the door handle only to find that it had already been locked. He pulled hard and frantic enough on the handle to snap it off, but the door wouldn't open. Mike leaned back from the door, pressing into the big guy in the passenger's seat.

Blankets of hot anger stifled David's ability to breath. He had to vent the wrath before it consumed him. In a frenzied act of need he kicked and punched at the door frame to try and get at the man who threatened him. He could scarcely think of anything else. The door, he realized soon enough, wouldn't open. That left one alternative.

He shattered the side window with his bare fists, feeling nothing of the cuts that would ultimately take hours to dress. Mike screamed for help as David reached in through the window and hauled him out of the car.

With the tenacity of a man who felt his very life was in danger, Mike struggled to free himself.

David would never let him escape, however. He had to destroy this danger before it destroyed him. Reasoning and common sense never set foot in the arena of a raging maniac. Instinct, not rationalization, fueled every move. David had plummeted into survival mode.

Unleashing his rage on the man in his grasp, David heard bones snap. He slammed the man's body into the car frame time and again, ignoring the pleas for mercy or for help. He pounded fists and elbows into the soft body of his enemy.

At length, Mike could scarcely move and David threw him on the ground in disgust, his anger and fear nowhere near spent. He didn't yet feel safe but he could no longer direct his anxieties toward this broken down threat.

He needed something else.

David circled the car to reach the other passenger and saw him still in the seat, wide-eyed and nearly crying. This man remained a threat. Still a danger.

David leaped onto the hood and began slamming into the windshield with his already bloodied fists. He had to get to the man who meant him harm. He had to eliminate him as well. If not, the man would rise up like a tidal wave and crush him like an insect. David had to protect himself.

With a frenzied rhythm, he crashed his fists down upon the unyielding windshield, cracking the glass in a thousand different places yet not able to open a hole large enough to reach and end the menace only a few feet away that waited to pounce and kill him.

The muscle-man in the car scratched and clawed his way over the seat, screaming that he wanted no part of this, that he wanted to be left out.

After seeing the desperation on the man's face and hearing him declare over and over that he had no intentions of harming him, David could ultimately calm down enough to stop. His breathing slowed, and his ability to think slowly returned. His hands stopped shaking.

Surveying the situation, he saw shattered glass covering the surrounding area. Streaks of blood drenched his hands and arms. Mike's car was a mess and Mike himself lay groaning and coughing up blood off in the distance. David estimated he'd probably broken at least four bones in the man's body.

A wave of all-too-familiar guilt and shame passed over him. Mike had certainly earned a whippin', though not like this. Nothing this bad. And as always, David hadn't been able to control himself. Mike would need to go to the hospital for sure.

David sat down on his bumper, brooding. How long until he paralyzed somebody in one of these fits of rage? How long until he killed someone? And all over a car.

Except he knew it had nothing to do with the car. This could have been over a single bottle of beer, or even nothing at all. The plain and simple fact was that someone had threatened him. The threat could have been real or it could have been a bluff, but in either case it would have still transformed David to a pillar of rage.

No matter how hard he tried, he couldn't seem to stop these lapses from happening. Two versions of himself constantly battled for control, and the animal inside only needed the slightest provocation to come full surface. It scared him as much now as it had for years.

Dad had stopped him from strangling Ina, although he knew there could arise other occasions when the rage might push him beyond his ability to hold back. He shuddered to think what might happen if he ever developed the same level of resentment and anger toward someone as he had with Ina. At the time he had been only fourteen or so; now he was a grown man. And what if nobody like Dad stopped him if that time ever came?

Though nearly twice his size, the guy in the car continued

to cower in the back seat, practically in tears and terrified that David would come after him anyway.

It had been ten years after his day in the courtroom in front of his schoolmates, and people still saw him as a freak.

"Take Mike to the hospital," David said numbly.

David walked to his car, anxious to leave before he did anything worse.

He started up the car and headed toward home. Kris would be able to take care of him. She would make the pain go away. She loved him. And Brinna and Eric would laugh and laugh as he tickled them and played with them. They loved him too. More than anything else in the world, he needed to feel loved at that moment.

Yet as he drove, the anguished details from his life seeped to the surface as they often did when his dark side came out. The courtroom testimony. Ina. Karl. All the nights as a child when he cried himself to sleep wondering if he would live to see another summer.

He realized that he couldn't go home right away. Not like that. Not with so many poisonous and dangerous emotions roiling within. Kris would understand. He couldn't bear to dump all of this on her. He had to unwind first. Plus, his little kids didn't need to see their daddy so upset.

Turning the car away from home, he headed back to the bar.

After stopping in the restroom to clean the blood off his hands and arms as best he could, he sat down at the bar stool weary and full of pain beyond that of his cuts and scrapes.

Cheston took one look at David's face and retrieved a glass without any of the usual small talk. He knew David well enough to not ask him any questions when he got like this. Once he tapped the usual draft into a tall mug and set it down quietly, he slipped away to other customers.

For a long time, David merely held the mug without sipping, fighting the demons inside that had by now risen to a fervored pitch. His hands sent signals of pain from the lacerations they had received, though David could scarcely detect the fact that he should be hurting in that way. A separate and distinct pain dwarfed the physical suffering he was in.

The emotional whirlwind had started in his own troubled mind, and he only knew one way to silence it. He had to quiet his mind.

He drank long and deep from the glass, the first of many he would undoubtedly consume before going home. His friends left him alone, recognizing that David had no intentions of drinking socially this night.

It was a night to bury pain.

Every man's work shall be made manifest: for the day shall declare it, because it shall be revealed by fire; and the fire shall try every man's work of what sort it is.

—1 Corinthians 3:13

# Chapter 13

David examined his knuckles as he gripped the steering wheel, grateful that the cuts on his hands from breaking Mike's windows had finally healed enough to stop people from asking about them. They didn't hurt, really, but he hated the attention. He feared that if his boss found out about how he had acquired them, he might fire David. After all, who wanted an employee who could go berserk at the drop of a hat?

Driving home from work, he tried to force out concerns of losing his job as he navigated the roads. And yet the thought kept returning, unwanted, to rattle around inside his head.

With all that he had to worry about as far as providing for his family, making payments on the new house, and so forth, the last thing he needed was to find himself out of work. He tried to rationalize that his boss liked him and that he wouldn't fire him over something that wasn't really his fault anyway, but it didn't help. Even though he could probably find another roofing job somewhere if he had to, seeing how practically nobody could keep up with his work pace, David still worried about finding enough money to cover everything.

He never seemed to earn enough to silence that concern. No matter how hard he worked or how much money he made, even if he could cover all of their bills, he remained convinced that the slightest possible surprise could cause him to lose everything. He could end up on the street with his wife and two little children, unable to keep food in their mouths or clothes on their backs.

A vivid image popped into his mind of his children crying with hunger and cold. The possibility of that actually happening struck David almost senseless. There seemed to him at all times a ravenous wolf lurking right outside their home. One tiny misstep would let the wolf in to destroy everything he loved.

These anxieties nearly paralyzed him. He could write down on a piece of paper his income, as well as their expenses, could see that the two matched up fine and yet it would offer him no comfort.

He worried about losing his job. He worried about when the kids grew older and required more money to care for them. And about the possibility of famine or war or anything that might prevent him from taking care of his family.

David could think of a hundred ways he could lose all that he cared about and could think of no way to adequately protect against them all.

He pulled into the driveway and trudged to the front door. From here he could see that Kris had left the light on in the front room with nobody in it, and he determined not to bring it up. He would simply flip off the light without mentioning anything about the cost of electricity.

After opening the front door, he automatically and against his better judgment checked the desk to see if Kris had paid the bills.

They sat staring at him menacingly. Untouched.

Kris came out from the kitchen and spread her arms wide to give him a hug. "Hi sweetie, how was your—"

"I thought you said you were going to pay the bills today?" David snapped.

Her face fell at his tone. "I'm sorry, the kids have had a hard day. Brinna still hasn't gotten over her cold. Eric's still cutting those two teeth. Don't worry, I'll pay them tomorrow."

David picked up the gas bill and pointed out a line to her. "See this date?"

"David, please. Not tonight."

"This date, Kris! Right here. The one in a big box at the top of the bill. That's in two days. How do you expect the check to reach them if you don't send it until tomorrow?"

Kris looked flustered. "So it will be a day late."

"Do you want them to turn off the gas? Do you?"

"That's not going to happen. At the most they'll give us a late fine."

"And how many of those do you think we can afford?"

Kris smoothed the folds of her dress, taking a deep breath.

"Come on, can we talk about this later? I said I'm sorry. Now I've made some dinner—"

David threw the bill down on the desk. "Why do I even bother asking you to handle these things?" He regretted the words as soon as he spoke them but he couldn't seem to take them back. He had slid into a form of auto pilot that he had come to hate, yet which he had no power to stop.

"Is it so hard to write a check, place it in the envelope, and mail the damn thing to the gas company?"

Kris stood in silence, resentment building on her face.

"Huh? Is that so hard?"

"I told you I would do it tomorrow," she said, her voice level. "What more do you want?"

David wished with all his might he could clamp his own jaw shut and say no more, but he couldn't control himself.

"I'll tell you what I want. I want you to get off your butt now and again and take care of a few simple things! Do I have two kids at home, or three?"

He could have ripped his own tongue out for saying that. No way in the world did Kris deserve such a cruel accusation. She took care of the household all day long. The kids were happy, they never went hungry, and they knew that they were loved. Kris even managed the bills perfectly fine, even if she occasionally sent one or two in late.

He loved Kris. He wanted to spend the rest of his life with her.

And yet he couldn't even treat her with the common courtesy she deserved.

She stared at him with eyes so full of hurt that he wanted to cry. "Dinner's in the oven if you're hungry."

With that, she stormed back to the bedroom.

"Kris, wait. Kris, I'm sorry."

But she had already disappeared into their room, slamming the door behind her.

Tears welled up in David's eyes. Why had he spoken to his wife like that?

The banging door woke Eric up. His one-year-old son still slept in their room. He could hear Kris picking him up and soothing him.

He heard another door open down the hall and saw three-year-old Brinna come out from her room. His beautiful daughter held a little toy horse in her hand.

"Hi, Daddy,"

David scooped her up, trying desperately to forget his behavior only moments earlier.

"Is you mad, Daddy?"

"No, sweetie."

Brinna looked into his eyes with the piercing honesty that only a little child can do.

"But you yelled."

"I know, honey. Mommy and Daddy were just having a grown-up talk. Now how would you like some tummy tickles?"

Brinna squealed as her daddy tickled her. For a brief moment, David's heart gladdened at her perfect laughter. He loved Brinna and Eric more fiercely than life itself. They made him happier than he could have imagined. Becoming a father had given him an anchor to cling to in the roughest of times.

Yet even as Brinna's magical laughter rang in his ears, he felt the stabs of guilt from his behavior earlier. The horrible regret blocked out almost all other emotions.

*Of course Kris could pay the bills tomorrow,* he chided himself. Truthfully, utilities went through tremendous efforts to collect money before shutting down a service. As for a late fee, it wouldn't even amount to a couple of drinks at the bar. Why had he flown off the handle? After all, Kris had told him the kids had had a hard day.

David did his best to withstand the rising tide of remorse while playing with his little girl for another half hour or so. He then sent her to bed with a glass of water and a hug.

He thanked God that his blackouts and lapses in control never extended to his children. If he would ever once lay a hand on them, no matter the reason, he didn't think he could live with himself afterward. Or if he laid a hand on Kris for that matter.

He was still perfectly capable of hurting Kris in other ways, though.

David slumped over on the couch in the silent house, wading through turmoil. He loved his family. He loved Kris, and yet he proved over and over again that he didn't deserve them. Kris had spent all day with the kids, one of whom was sick, and the other of whom was teething. Even so, she still found time to fix dinner. She had probably reached her wits end before he'd come home and needed some comfort herself. And how had he repaid her loving efforts? With an impulsive fit over something that didn't amount to more than a couple glasses of beer.

The blade of regret twisted another turn in his heart.

Sitting on the couch, David absorbed the quiet of his house for a long time agonizing over his harsh and uncalled-for conduct. Kris must have decided to retire to bed early rather than come back out and face him.

Though he had little appetite, he determined to try the dinner if only so he could thank her for it later. He found in the oven one of his favorite casseroles. Just enough of the meal was missing to account for Brinna and Eric's dinner. Kris had obviously waited to eat hers with him when he got home. The extra measure of guilt at realizing that Kris had gone to bed hungry prohibited him from taking a single bite.

At length he tiptoed down the hall and into their bedroom. He could tell from her breathing that she had not yet fallen to sleep.

They could have had a good evening. He ruined it.

"Kris, are you awake?" He knew she was, but he didn't know if she would answer.

"You know I am."

"Kris . . . I'm so sorry. I can't believe what I said. That wasn't fair."

She said nothing in response.

"Please forgive me?" he asked. He wanted to drop on his knees and beg her to do so.

"I need you to forgive me, Kris, even though I don't deserve it." If she couldn't forgive him, he didn't know how he would cope.

She lay in stillness a few moments longer before taking a deep breath.

"I always do," she replied at last.

David lay down next to her and wanted to hold her close but couldn't with the emotions churning inside. He had so many things he wanted to say to her, though he kept them all inside for fear of making things worse somehow if he let them out.

He couldn't trust himself to do anything but remain there in the quiet of the night. He loved this woman. And yet more often than he cared to admit when he opened his mouth he'd say things to her that he later came to regret. He feared that any touch right then, any word, would lead to another unforeseen but regrettable consequence.

The wolf outside was the animal within himself, David realized with a start. The person he struggled so hard to suppress would be the same creature to destroy this family if he couldn't control it.

He renewed his resolve to keep that hideous monster far, far from sight. He would give it no chances to cause any more destruction than it already had.

Laying side by side in the same bed and in the same room,

David thought he and Kris might as well be in two different places entirely. He couldn't feel close to her. Not after what he had said and done.

Maybe an hour passed before her soft and steady breathing indicated that she'd fallen asleep. Married couples had arguments, he reminded himself. No marriage was perfect. After all, he had been rude and unfair, but at least he hadn't screamed and swore at her or insulted her in any truly horrible way. She would forget about it by the morning, and he would certainly not act that selfishly again. That should fix everything

So why did he feel so thoroughly awful?

Oily snakes of remorse tightened their scaly bodies around him with constant force. He pictured the wolf again, lurking nearby. The realization that he himself was that creature did little to calm David. The predator waited, regardless, for an opportunity to destroy his little family.

He feared that darker side to himself above all else. Tonight Kris had forgiven him. But how long would she continue to tolerate his outbursts?

The emotional spiral continued to suck him down. The more concerned he grew about losing what he valued, the more he appeared to slip and stumble in trying to keep it. He wondered how he might possibly enjoy a future with such horrible flaws constantly at his heels. Though he would pay any price to change his nature, the ugly memories and pain from his past forever wreaked havoc inside, leaving little possibility for peace of mind.

Several hours later, when sleep could not have strayed further from David's body, he slipped out of bed. The guilt wouldn't relent. His relatively small outburst to Kris had by degrees grown into some colossal and devastating event inside his mind. He feared not so much what happened as he feared what may yet happen. He knew he'd never grow violent with his loved ones, no matter the occasion, but a wolf only needed to bare its teeth long and often enough to frighten others away. Just how long could they put up with him?

Before leaving the bedroom, he checked little Eric's crib. Eric slept so peacefully. How powerfully David loved his son. There was so much he wanted to teach him. How to roof, how to start a campfire, how to fish, and a thousand other things. David would do better. He would keep the wolf at bay. He wouldn't lose his little family.

With that renewed resolve, he shut the bedroom door quietly behind him.

He needed to clear his head. If he intended to show up for work—and he always did—David wanted at least a couple hours of sleep. The bars were closed at this hour, although he kept a bottle or two of whisky around for just such occasions. Before going to the pantry, he cracked open the door to Brinna's room. How he loved her perfect laughter, her beautiful smile. Her hugs could take the chill off the iciest day. He would do better for her too, and for Kris.

He could conquer his demons for his loved ones. He *could*.

As he entered into the pantry, his demons seemed to laugh.

It is easy to go down into Hell; night and day, the gates of
dark death stand wide; but to climb back again, to retrace
one's steps to the upper air—there's the rub, the task.

—Virgil

# Chapter 14

"We went on like that for several years, Alice. I continued to mess things up even when I wanted with all my heart to be a good husband and father."

Alice listened attentively, leaning forward on the park bench.

"You see, we had plenty of love—in fact, the love was quite powerful for me because it took the place of all the bad that happened in the past—but I didn't have the tools to make the marriage functional. No matter how desperately I wanted things to work, I kept unintentionally chiseling away at our marital foundation. One particularly destructive method was my drinking.

"For example, a typical night would be for me to get off work and then the guy I worked for would want to go grab a beer. I'd try to back out of it but he'd say, 'Naw, come on, you can have one and go home.'

"So, I'd give in, and when I'd show up and run into my buddies, I'd call home and tell Kris to expect me a few minutes late. Then I wouldn't go home for three or four hours, which always made me feel guilty when I finally did walk through the door."

David still experienced remorse when he recalled those days, even though they were long behind him.

"I always felt guilty over something, even if I couldn't pin down why I felt that way. I'd go home from the bar, begging her to forgive me, and she would. I constantly felt torn, though, questioning if I did the right thing, the wrong thing, or what? I knew I loved her and that I loved my kids, I just didn't know where all this pain came from."

"That sounds like a horrible way to live," Alice said.

David nodded. "I was always so tied up in knots that I never really experienced much of the marriage. I simply hurt all the time from the pain inside. I literally suffered every day. I'd get up in the morning and feel miserable the moment my eyes opened. I was terrible to be around. I don't know how anybody could have lived with me."

"So how long did you two stay married?"

"The official divorce didn't happen until we'd been married about ten years, but our marriage was in serious trouble long before that."

David stood to stretch his muscles a bit before continuing.

"It all started to go downhill pretty quickly after she landed a job at the same bar where my mom used to work. Kris finally found a place to make a buck on her own and so one day she finally had enough of me. I didn't even see it coming. She just said, 'I want you outta here.'

"It floored me. I didn't have wisdom or knowledge, and I had always been a very jealous man, so I immediately thought she said this because she was doing something wrong, cheating on me and stuff, which she wasn't doing at all. The fact was that everything in our marriage had built up to that moment. All my ghosts came back to haunt me at once. I just didn't see 'em coming until they smacked me in the face."

Alice seemed a little sad. "So then what happened?"

"We separated off and on for a year or two, at first. We'd stay apart for a while and then she'd call and say we gotta get back together, that she missed me, and so forth. It never worked out, but it dragged on for a long time. We wanted to be together, yet we didn't know how. We were just miserable, both of us."

Alice started rubbing her hands to warm them.

David suddenly realized how long they'd been outside. "Do you need to head back?"

"No, no. I'm fine. It's nice to have some fresh air for a change. Please continue."

David liked that she wanted to stay out of the Braxton house despite the chill in the air. It showed that she could tell that place was no good for her.

"Well, after we'd separated for a while, Kris started dating this other guy. That caused me more jealousy than I could handle. Even though our marriage had long since turned for the worse, seeing her move on to another man nearly killed me. I had to leave town. Seeing how it was winter at the time and I couldn't work around home until the snow melted, I chose to take a couple of buddies with me to Vegas to go roofing for a few months.

"I didn't know it at the time, but when I pointed my truck toward Las Vegas, I was heading for a major turning point in my life."

The Nevada desert presented absolutely no variation in landscape as the hours dragged by on the open road. It felt to David like he was trapped in some science fiction movie where he drove the same stretch of road over and over without realizing it. A little mini-time-warp. For someone used to living around mountains his whole life, the monotony in landscape had a pretty disorienting effect.

"We outta beef jerky?" Chad asked.

"Almost," Marcus answered. "And it's your turn to buy some more."

David groaned. He'd had more than his fill of travel snacks these past two days. The first thing he wanted to do when they arrived was hit one of those fancy buffets Chad kept talking about. Chad had been to Vegas before and was the only one of the three who had. He said it was a pretty exciting town, but

David had his doubts. He wondered how such a dry and barren place could be anything but boring.

And since they were now only an hour or so away from Vegas, the terrain couldn't change all that much before they arrived. Even here in the beginning of winter it looked like the ground hadn't seen rain in months.

Not that he was coming down here to sightsee, David reminded himself. For all he cared, the ground could consist of solid gravel and asphalt for miles on end. As long as Vegas stayed warm enough for him to keep working and away from home for a few months, it would suit him fine.

Picturing Kris dating another man nearly made his blood boil every time he thought about it. He needed a vacation from everything. He couldn't stand the thought of hanging around home all winter long, idling away his time while watching Kris from a distance. Besides, he had always wanted to go to Vegas.

Thoughts of Brinna and Eric floated up to him. She was now eight, and Eric six. *They had had such fun camping last summer. Eric had caught that huge old fish and Brinna had had so much fun roasting s'mores like she always did. Maybe next year they could—*

David stopped that train of thought. He knew that no matter how much he loved his kids, the best thing for the whole family was for him to leave town for a few months and let things blow over. Get his head straight.

*Stop thinking about Kris,* he chided himself, and then pressed the accelerator even harder.

He was glad he'd brought Marcus and Chad along. They had nothing better to do for a few months anyway. He'd enjoy their company in this strange new city.

About a half hour later, David saw the lights of the city in the dusk.

"Now that's what I call wild," Marcus said.

David had to admit the sight was pretty remarkable. He'd visited a couple larger cities, but nothing like this. The desert literally seemed on fire with electricity. A bright glow surrounded each building like a huge, transparent cloud.

"Gentlemen," Chad said excitedly, "get ready for the time of your lives!"

Though his friends whooped and laughed about all that lay before them, something about the enormity of the city in front of him started to fill David with a sense of nervous anticipation. He couldn't turn back now, he knew, but he also began to wonder if maybe coming here had been a mistake after all.

David looked around the casino. Chad had been right. This town never slept. Never once in these past several months since they'd come here had he needed to stop and think. If he wasn't working, he was partying. And there were more women in Vegas than he knew what to do with.

A small part of him whispered, as he scanned the roulette tables for his next conquest, that he was still a married man, but he didn't pay the voice any heed. Too many beautiful women called for his attention instead.

He had to admit that for all its excitement, the town did grate on him at times. It was a small price to pay for the escape Vegas provided, but still—the constant ringing of slot machines, the ever-present glowing neon lights, the millions of people wandering around with hardly anybody really caring for each other. The sirens, the traffic . . .

He cleared his head. So what if there were sirens? He came to this place to have fun. He could go back to his uneventful town soon enough.

Tonight, he had business to attend to.

David had developed a knack for conquering the best-looking woman in the building. Nothing less would do. He scanned the crowd for her, trying to find the most stunning girl around to win over. Not a prostitute, of course. They didn't count. No challenge involved with them. Nothing to conquer.

He spotted her. A gorgeous brunette with all the right curves stood near the blackjack table, practically daring any man with blood in his veins not to stare. David downed another shot of whisky and sauntered over. She arched an eyebrow at his approach. This sort of woman would be no stranger to men's attention. She clearly wondered what this newcomer had to offer.

David walked right up to her and brushed his hair back in an easy manner.

"I bet you're wondering what I'm going to say to you," he said.

The girl blinked in surprise.

Shrugging his shoulders, he continued. "Well, nothing, actually. I just thought I'd give you a shot to try out your best line on me."

She said nothing for a few moments, apparently trying to figure out if she should laugh or scowl. David glanced at his watch.

"Time's up."

He turned to leave and hadn't made it four steps before she called him back, laughing.

"You've got guts," she said. "Buy me a drink. My name's Carrie."

David smiled. He knew from experience that it was all downhill from there.

Thanks to the incredibly thick curtains, Carrie's bedroom remained blissfully dark despite the neon signs right outside of her window. Darkness was too rare a thing in this electrically overdosed city. Carrie slept soundlessly next to him in her oversized bed. David, however, could not fall asleep despite the idealistic conditions of her bedroom.

It was this city that kept him awake. More importantly, what the city did to him. The turmoil outside the walls of the apartment couldn't compare to the unrest inside his own mind. David tried not to hyperventilate. His breathing had already grown so loud and rapid that Carrie began to stir awake next to him.

No matter how hard he worked, how hard he partied, or how busy he kept himself, he still could not escape these terrifying moments of quietude. And, as ironic as it seemed, the perpetual chaos of Las Vegas only made the silent moments all the more impossible to endure. He'd started sleeping less and less each night, pushing himself at work and at play until he literally passed out from exhaustion.

Tonight he should have already passed out as he often did, but the anxiety was especially bad. He felt the attack coming on full swing, forcing him to drop out of bed and call it quits for the night. He could go another day without sleep. It's not like he hadn't done it before.

Holding still while the weight of the universe crushed against his skull, however, was not something he felt up to at the moment. He tried not to notice how frequently these anxiety attacks struck lately.

Attempting not to wake his new acquaintance, David snuck out of the bedroom and down the stairs as quietly as he could.

"I thought I heard someone open the bedroom door," a voice said.

The woman standing in the downstairs kitchen caught David by surprise. He had thought Carrie lived alone in this apartment.

"I'm Carrie's mother," she explained.

David noticed through her clinging nightgown that she still possessed a very attractive body for her age and then dismissed the absurd observation. She was at least a good twenty years older than him.

"Tell her I couldn't sleep," David said.

The woman smiled mischievously. "Oh, I think I'll come up with something a bit more creative than that. Don't want her getting too attached to you."

David couldn't guess what she meant by that, but decided not to ask. At the moment he wanted nothing other than to leave the building. Try his hand at cards, perhaps. Play the one-armed bandits. Keep busy. He couldn't go to work for at least a few more hours. But that was the beauty of Vegas. As Chad had said, the city never slept. Why should he?

As he walked past Carrie's mother and out the front door, he thought he saw her wink.

Two mornings later David lay awake in his own bed, tormented with despair. Knots of anguish so thoroughly coiled about him that he wanted to die.

He rolled over and saw her again in the dimly lit room. Carrie's mother. He had never learned her name. She snored softly in his bed.

David took stock of his situation. He had done a lot of stupid things in his life, but this defied even his own track record. Was this all his life would become? A series of mind-numbing adventures? Conquering one lady after another? One party after another?

He had a clear picture of his life stretching out in front of him. He saw himself waking up day after day, barely remembering the person in bed next to him. And spending his evenings at wild parties, drinking and dancing—all in an effort to hide his pain behind a few pleasures.

Jumping out of bed, he dashed to the bathroom and threw some cold water on his face. Many times he'd been surprised by his own reflection in the past. But not until today had he ever seen an old man in the mirror.

The man glaring back at him over the sink looked closer to fifty than his actual twenty-seven. Heavy bags lined his eyes. He had probably slept a total of ten hours in the past four days. And no matter who the woman was, no matter the liquor, no matter his success at the card table, his personal problems only seemed to grow stronger.

He could see no end to this bottomless pit he'd fallen into.

*There has to be more to life than this,* he reasoned. He had to find something else. If not, then he might as well die right then and there.

A strange resolve crept over him as he stared in the mirror. It came slowly at first, and then in a rush. Indeed, there *had* to be something better out there.

He'd pretty well exhausted the possibilities of finding happiness in a bar or casino. Wherever he had to go, whatever he had to do, he would not stop until he knew what life was supposed to be about. He would be a better father to his kids, if nothing else.

For the first time in his life, David felt he could stare his own demons right in the eyes and tell them to go back to hell where they belonged. He would remain their slave no longer, or he would die fighting them. Yes, he would sooner die than fall another inch into this dark hole.

David had no clue where things would end up, but he knew one thing for certain. He had to leave Las Vegas. If he didn't find a way to calm his tempest of a life, his heart would fail him anyway. And Vegas did anything but calm him.

Without another moment to consider the implications, he stormed back into his bedroom and threw open the curtains. Carrie's mother squirmed in protest at the bright light.

"Get out," he said.

She stretched and smiled playfully. "Mmm. How about you come back to bed instead? I'd like to pick up where we—"

"Now!" He threw her clothes at her.

The woman scowled at his tone. "I think you're forgetting who invited who here, David."

She dressed in a hurry and stomped to the front door.

"Don't bother coming around the casino any more!" she yelled back while leaving.

David slammed the door behind her. Now there was a request he would have no problem fulfilling. He picked up the phone.

"Marcus, I'm going home," he announced. "Yes, today."

He hadn't been out of Vegas for more than two hours before he started to relax for the first time in weeks. He pressed the accelerator. The quicker he could leave Vegas behind, the better. Soon he could see Brinna and Eric and give them both hugs and kisses. He'd file for divorce with Kris immediately, though. Time to close the book on that painful chapter in his life.

He'd stop drinking, or at least slow down. He would learn to control his temper.

Things would change, and that could only mean things would improve.

Chad and Marcus decided to stay a bit longer since they had nothing to go home to anyway. Roofing couldn't start for another few weeks at the soonest. They'd arrange a ride home some other way.

David didn't blame them. They needed the money. So did he, for that matter. But he wouldn't stay in that place another minute. He could live the rest of his life without setting foot in Vegas and that wouldn't bother him one bit.

As the miles flew by, David wondered what sort of life he would be driving home to. Earlier that morning something had snapped inside of him—a wake up call of major proportions. He couldn't tell yet what that meant. For all he knew, it indicated that he simply didn't have the strength to go on living any more. Maybe he'd die within a few months after all.

But if there was something else out there, he'd find it. One way or another, life would not stay the same. He'd be happy, or he'd be dead.

He smiled as he drove, feeling a hint of hope for himself and the future.

Vegas gave him a pretty good glimpse of how not to live, he realized. The neon city basically allowed him to see his life for what it had truly become. A complete wreck.

*No longer,* he promised himself, though he had no idea how to fulfill that promise.

A rest-stop sign grabbed his attention and David's weariness caught up with him in the span of a few seconds. No way could he drive home without some sleep. It was mid-morning, but he pulled off the road anyway. He scarcely had time to pull his car under a shade tree before he fell fast asleep.

✦ ✦ ✦

Home. David lay awake on a couch at his friend's house in the middle of the night. Unlike similar bouts of insomnia in Las Vegas, David lay awake this time from excitement, not dread.

It had surprised David when, earlier that week, he'd driven back into his town and felt so thrilled to see it. Snow had still covered the ground and the quiet town still slept, but it had never looked better. He remembered tearing up at the sight. And seeing his two kids again felt like a breath of fresh air.

Following through on his intentions, the divorce was already underway. It took a tremendous amount of courage to go into the city office and file, though he continued to look to the future with hope.

He tried not to think about how often he may or may not see his kids when all the dust settled.

Now, laying on his friend's couch in the dead of night, David began to plan out the details of how he would begin to put his life back together. He could always move away from everything and get a fresh start somewhere else. Then again, he liked where he lived. Maybe he could start his own roofing business instead of always working for somebody else.

Further, he knew he had to stop drinking as often. The old bar-hopping habits wouldn't help his new life much. And maybe he should consider doing some kind of community service. Visiting kids in hospitals or something. *Whatever it takes,* he reminded himself.

Suddenly, David heard a little burst of wind and the room went instantly cold. A completely foreign and powerful dark feeling came over him. A feeling that had nothing to do with anxiety. He could scarcely breath. Pure hate seemed to cut against his flesh as though by barbed wire.

His body actually sunk further into the couch cushions, pressed by an unseen force.

This power, saturated with evil and fueled by anger, felt strong enough to tear him limb from limb.

Soon David could not breath at all. His lungs refused to move. He tried to throw himself off the couch and crawl for help but his entire body was rigid. Locked tight.

Even if he could have reached the telephone, he had no intentions of calling for an ambulance. This was no heart attack.

Abject terror filled him to overflowing. Never in his life had he felt more scared. Something was being done to him by one with intelligence and cunning.

Tears fell down David's cheeks as he continued to fight for breath. The fear inside and all around threatened to tear his sanity from him once and for all. No man could fight such a power.

In times past, David had always wanted to tear something apart when his emotions became this severe.

Now, however, he wanted to cower in a corner and cry. He had no fire in him, only desperation. His lungs burned for want of oxygen, yet he remained powerless to draw in air.

And then, unbidden, the thought came to him to pray. He hadn't prayed since he was a child, but he didn't hesitate to try. If he didn't, he knew he would not survive this encounter.

*Please God, help me. I don't want to die yet.*

He couldn't utter the words out loud, so he'd spoken them in his heart. No sooner had he finished his petition than the force left him entirely. He choked in deep breaths of air while lying on the ground shaking. Tears gushed down his cheeks as he tried to compose himself.

The bedroom door flew open and Derek came running out, looking fervently around the living room for David could only guess what.

David expected Derek to ask him why he was thrashing around on the ground like that. He knew also that he could never adequately describe what had happened.

But when he saw Derek's face and the naked fear in it, David knew he wouldn't have to explain himself. His friend was terrified, not confused.

As David sat up, composing himself and catching his breath, Derek finally found his voice.

"You felt it, didn't you?" Derek asked.

David merely nodded. There was no need to ask what he meant. Even with the lights left on to reassure them, neither of them could sleep for the remainder of the night.

But every man is tempted, when he is drawn away of his own lust, and enticed. Then when lust hath conceived, it bringeth forth sin: and sin, when it is finished, bringeth forth death.

—James 1: 14-15

# Chapter 15

Even though he had already pretty much filled himself up with whisky, David decided to poke his head into his favorite bar. With over a month home from Vegas and only a handful of drinking trips since then, he had certainly earned this night. Besides, whatever dark feeling had come over him at Derek's apartment seemed to leave him alone in here . . .

He only wanted to say hi to some buddies anyway.

The crowd greeted him warmly when he came in.

"Hey, David, what'll it be?" asked the bartender.

"Oh hell, gimme the usual." One more would be fine, he reasoned. He had already cut way back on his drinking.

He heard some talking at the other table. A stray piece of the conversation reached his ears. "Jeanie Hancock's gettin' divorced," somebody said.

Jeanie Hancock. The name hit him quite forcefully, though he couldn't say why. David had never met her and had only vaguely seen her around a little bit. As the other men continued talking about her, the strangest feeling came over him. He realized something right then and there that amazed him beyond description. He couldn't begin to explain how he knew this, he just did.

He walked over to the table to share the recent discovery. "Boys, I'm gonna marry her!" They looked at him as though he'd sprouted cauliflower out his eye sockets. "Jeanie Hancock," he said again. "I'm gonna marry her."

Jeanie's brother sat at the table. "You're drunker'n a skunk, David. You ain't even met her. And Jeanie wouldn't go out with someone like you."

Smiling by way of reply, David checked his watch. Nearly eleven. Not too late to call. He finished his beer and hustled out of the bar, excited to get home and look up Jeanie Hancock. He wanted to laugh. This sounded crazy, even for him. Still, he didn't care. He knew what he felt back there. He was going to marry this girl.

But first he had to meet her.

He drove to his apartment and grabbed a phone book. When he found her number, he checked his watch again. A little after eleven. She might be asleep. Oh well, he figured. He'd wake her up anyway. He had a good reason.

The phone rang a few times at the other end before a groggy voice answered.

"Hello?"

David grinned. Yup, he'd marry her all right. "Hi, is this Jeanie Hancock?"

"Yes," she replied, still sounding a little sleepy. "Who is this?"

"David Briggs. I'm taking you out on a date. When can you go?"

It had taken two hours the previous night before she'd finally relented in the phone call and agreed to go out with him, and David counted those two hours well spent.

For their date, they had gone to dinner and a movie. The whole night was rather ordinary with respect to the food they ate, the movie they watched, and the conversations they had. Even so, all throughout the date David couldn't stop smiling and wondering why this one date should feel so different from all the other first dates he'd been on.

Now, after dropping her off and saying good night, David experienced a lightness spread through him. He practically leaped down the front steps to his car. She seemed to radiate goodness and happiness. He couldn't pin down what made her so unique from other girls he'd dated. He only knew that he wanted to find out. Simply being around her made him happy.

He checked his watch again. Nearly midnight. Some of the boys would still be in the bar. He parked the car and hopped out, running up to the door and poked his head in.

"Mark my words, boys!" he yelled. "I'm going to marry that girl!" They laughed, figuring the whole thing a joke, and David let them. They'd find out soon enough. He shut the door once again and hopped back into his car, feeling happier inside than he had in years.

He had promised himself before meeting Jeanie that he would never marry a girl until he had dated her at least a year. True to his promise, a little over a year after their first date, they had been married by the justice of the peace at a no-frills wedding in the courthouse.

They used no flowers or decorations for the occasion. The only guests were his two kids and Jeanie's two kids, Justin and Jason. Her boys, close in age to his own children, would be living with Jeanie and himself.

David had never felt more right about any decision he'd ever made. He would enjoy this new life of his, even if it required that he make a few changes in his lifestyle.

For one thing, he would continue to stay away from drinking. Several months earlier, he had bet Marcus that he couldn't go a week without drinking. Marcus had bet him right back. David didn't last two days. Since that time, he realized he had a bit of a drinking problem and had cut back almost completely.

David took a quick stock of his life. He drank less, had married a woman who made him feel like a new man, and had plans to start his own business. He stayed completely loyal in his relationship with Jeanie. He didn't have fights any more. The anxiety attacks came a lot less frequently. Things were looking up.

Shortly before they had been married a year, some old buddies showed up and wanted to take David drinking, for old time's sake.

Jeanie scowled at David's decision to go along. "I really don't want you to do this, David."

"Oh, come on. I haven't gone out with the guys in forever."

"David!"

He waved off the protests. It had been so long. He had definitely earned a night with his friends after cutting back for so long. Life couldn't be all work and no play. He'd make it up to her.

Long after he'd finished up the night with his buddies and had come home, in the small hours of the morning David began to feel a pain in his lower back. Jeanie no doubt had fallen asleep by now and he didn't want to wake her up by staggering in drunk, so he'd tried sleeping on the couch.

Now at three in the morning he still couldn't fall asleep because of this unusual back pain. He'd be wasted tired tomorrow for sure. What a great time they'd had tonight, though. He'd have to do that a little more often. It couldn't hurt to go out now and again. Not even in this new life of his. A little wind-down time at the end of the work day.

He finally began drifting off to sleep when another sharp pain in his lower back brought him fully awake. He staggered to the kitchen to grab an ice pack. This pain confused him. He couldn't remember tweaking his back at work, although he obviously had. He'd probably lifted something heavy, or twisted around too far. It'd go away soon enough.

Except it didn't. It only worsened as the day wore on.

Later that day, David lay writhing on a hospital bed. He had long since learned to endure pain that would put most men in the doctor's office, but this surpassed even his threshold. If someone had stabbed a knife in his lower back and twisted it around every half-minute or so, it wouldn't have hurt any less.

"How do you feel?" the doctor asked.

"Like a knife is in my back," David answered, using the words that had just barely been rolling around in his head. He could think of no better way to explain it. Jeanie stood by the bed, anxious, holding David's hand. The doctor consulted some blood work results.

"I'm sure it's an inflammation of the muscle from overwork," he said. "The tests don't show anything unusual." He scribbled off a prescription. "Here. Take these anti-inflammatories and let me know if things don't improve. Try to take it easy for a few days."

Jeanie took two steps closer to the doctor. "My husband once ran over his foot with a lawn mower and didn't bother telling anybody about it until they noticed the bloody footprints."

David blinked. He didn't remember telling her that story.

"So you might say he can deal with pain," she continued. "And now you'd like me to believe his muscles are merely inflamed?" She pointed a finger at David while continuing to speak to the doctor. "I've never seen him like this. You'd better check those tests again!"

The doctor held his hands up in protest. "I'm sorry, ma'am. That's how I see it. If the medicines don't help, you're always free to come back for another diagnosis."

"We won't be coming back," she said. "You're not competent enough for us to bother."

David watched his wife in awe. He always knew her no-non-sense ways and tough-as-nails character could intimidate others when she brought it out. Until then, however, he had never fully seen it. The doctor adjusted his stethoscope for lack of anything better to do.

"The pharmacy will be open for another hour," he said. "I'll send a nurse in to help you to your car." The doctor scowled and set the prescription on the table before leaving.

Jeanie watched him go, breathing deeply, barely restraining herself from yelling.

"Jeanie, let's at least try the prescription," David said. "He *is* a doctor."

"Fine," she conceded. "And when the meds don't help, we go to a specialist. This guy couldn't diagnose a missing arm."

The next day he grew worse by the minute. He didn't think such a thing possible. He could scarcely hear Jeanie on the phone through all the pain. In frantic tones she spoke with a doctor who's name she had obtained from a friend of theirs. A specialist.

Then he heard Jeanie gasp. She quickly ended the conversation and hung up the phone.

"David, Dr. Lilenquist just got your blood work from the other clinic. I'm driving you to the hospital. Now."

David could barely recall afterward much of the drive to the hospital except that every time Jeanie made a turn the pain in his back seemed to double for a brief moment. The hospital rushed him in to see the doctor as soon as they arrived. Dr. Lilenquist immediately struck them both as a kind and competent doctor. He had put Jeanie right at ease, David noticed. That was a good sign.

The pain in his back finally began to ebb a little, although David didn't like all the IV's hooked up to him. He hoped they would come out soon. He listened attentively as Dr. Lilenquist referred to his clipboard.

"There are certain enzymes in the blood that can indicate disease in the body," he explained. "One of them is lisame. We test the blood for the lisame enzyme count, among other things. To help you understand, we would consider a normal level about two hundred units per liter. That count would indicate a healthy pancreas, among other things."

"There's something wrong with his pancreas?" Jeanie asked, nervous.

David didn't know much about medicine but didn't like the direction of this conversation so far.

The doctor nodded. "Elevated levels of the lisame enzyme can start pointing to drastic problems. A count over eight hundred should be fatal." He lowered the clipboard and took off his glasses. "David, your lisame count is nearly a thousand."

Jeanie's voice cracked. "Does . . . this mean that—"

The doctor hastened to calm her. "No, no. I'm sorry to startle you. He will be fine."

David and Jeanie took a relieved breath.

Dr. Lilenquist pointed to the equipment. "We've stabilized the threat. He will recover. You should know, however, that such a high lisame enzyme count points to pancreatitis."

As David met eyes with the doctor, he saw some disbelief in the man's face. Not disbelief as to whether David would pull through—he thought the doctor spoke the truth on that count—but disbelief that David hadn't already died. The thought made him cringe. Not every day did a medical doctor regard his patient with awe simply because their heart still beat.

"This has some implications on lifestyle habits, which we'll talk about later," the doctor said. "First, though, we need to take some pretty drastic measures to get you back to full health.

"Could you tell me the last thing you ate, David?"

David searched his memory. "I think a couple handfuls of stale potato chips."

The doctor shook his head. "What a shame. Too bad it wasn't a nice steak dinner, or something equally tasty. The memory of those potato chips will have to last you for a couple weeks."

"Why?" David asked, though he feared he knew the answer.

"Say hello to your breakfast, lunch, and dinner," the doctor said, tapping the IV line. "Your pancreas has sustained severe damage. It can't heal if it's being used. And that means no food whatsoever."

"I'll starve!" David protested.

"No you won't, though truthfully you might think you will. You'll get plenty of calories through the IV line."

The doctor turned to Jeanie. "I need you to promise me that you won't go soft on him. No sneaking in any food for him, no matter how much he begs."

"No worries there," Jeanie said. "I promise."

Dr. Lilenquist nodded. "David, this will be a rough ride, but you'll get through it. You're lucky to be alive. And now," he said, facing Jeanie. "I think he needs some rest."

"One more question please," Jeanie said. "The other hospital, that arrogant doctor we saw the first time, did he have this information in front of him?"

For a few seconds Dr. Lilenquist scratched his head while searching for the right words.

"Unless you know what to look for, it can be overlooked easy enough."

"Doctor," she said, an edge to her voice.

At length he sighed. "Yes. He did. The count wasn't as high then as it is now, yet even then it scored way over safe levels. I've already arranged to speak with him tomorrow morning. He will have no excuse good enough for missing such a result."

He turned to David. "Remember, no matter how rough the recovery, you'll be getting better."

Two weeks later, David decided the doctor had flat out lied about the recovery process not killing him. He'd lost twenty pounds and felt like the hospital staff were slowly starving him to death, drawing out the torture as long as they possibly could. *This couldn't be medicine,* he rationalized.

And he had begged Jeanie for even a few crackers. All in vain. She had sided with the doctor and wouldn't even walk into the room if she had snacks of any kind on her person. She was every bit as ruthless as the staff.

Dr. Lilenquist walked into the room and perused the latest test results. David cringed for the inevitable. 'Not quite there yet,' the doctor would say again, and the torture would continue.

"Looking great, David," the doctor said one day. "I think it's time to send you home."

David couldn't believe his ears. "Really?"

"Yes," Dr. Lilenquist said, smiling. "Turns out we weren't trying to kill you after all, I suppose."

"So I can eat and everything?"

The doctor handed David a sheet of paper. While reading it

over, he had to stifle a few swear words. Doctor Lilenquist had prescribed for him a dietary recovery process starting out with broths and soups. He couldn't have any decent food for at least another couple weeks.

"I gave your wife a copy of this last week," the doctor said. "She intends to follow it to the letter. Your pancreas needs time to come up to speed again."

Even though David felt slightly cheated, the prospect of having anything at all in his stomach overwhelmed him with eager anticipation. He could do this. Besides, he had expected some form of restriction or another. Going from an empty stomach to a pork roast and potatoes dinner was hoping for too much.

The doctor removed his glasses again and fixed a very serious stare on David. "Before I unhook your lines, David, we need to have a talk."

David nodded hesitantly, not liking the doctor's tone.

"If you cheat on the little dietary chart I've given you, at most you'll experience some discomfort. Bloating, cramps, stuff like that. Make no mistake, you won't want to do this. I'm simply being honest with you. Nothing serious will likely happen, other than some mild pain."

Fantastic news, David thought. He already began plotting out how and where he would cheat on this rabbit-food diet.

"Now, I need to ask you something," the doctor said. "Do you have any idea what the typical pancreatitis patient profile is?"

David shrugged. "No, not really."

"Elderly people mostly," he answered. "Most of whom are overweight and physically inactive."

Strange news, David thought. Though he sensed something else in store.

"So I'm not a normal case, then?"

He shook his head. "Not at all. In fact, I've got to be frank, here. There's a pretty good reason your first doctor missed the diagnosis. Inexcusable, yes, but still a good reason." He spread his hands wide. "David, you're just too young for it. Too young, too tough, and far too healthy to fit that profile. Many doctors honestly wouldn't even think to check for it, in your case."

"That's interesting." David could think of nothing else to say. He didn't like the way the doctor scrutinized him. He hadn't said everything he intended to yet, David knew. He braced for the rest of it.

"Interesting," the doctor repeated. "Yes, to say the least. Now I spared you the stern talk on the diet because I don't want you in any way to take lightly what I say next."

*Here it comes,* David thought.

"While I can't begin to understand how this happened to someone as healthy as you, I can make you one promise." Dr. Lilenquist leaned forward for emphasis and spoke the words David feared to hear more than almost any others. "If you drink again, you will die."

Doctor Lilenquist's words from several months ago rose up in warning as David set foot into the bar. But he hadn't come to drink, he reminded himself. He only wanted to see his friends. It had been a stressful week at work.

Even Jeanie wouldn't deny him a little association with his friends.

"Hey, David!" Marcus called over. Chad sat next to him. "I thought you weren't supposed to drink no more."

He approached his friends. "I ain't here to drink. I can still hang out with my friends, can't I?"

They were more than willing to let him join their table. As they sat talking about the good old days, David began to wonder if Doctor Lilenquist had only been using scare tactics on him.

His pancreas had been healing for three months. He even flubbed on that dietary schedule and developed nothing more than a little gas. Nothing at all, really. The doc must have meant that long-term, serious drinking would kill him. Not one night of it. And certainly not one single beer.

He reached across the table for one, and Chad eyed him nervously. "Hey, David, are you sure you should be doin' that?"

"Oh, don't worry about that whole doctor thing. He only said to cut back and all," David lied. Except he hadn't really told a lie, he realized. The more he thought about it, the more he realized that the doctor had meant a *life* of drinking would kill him, not a few drinks.

"Really?" Marcus asked. "I sorta thought it was worse than that. Like you're body couldn't take it or something."

"Naw," David reassured them. "I only need to tone it down a little. Not go as often. At least not as often as the two of you, anyway."

Chad and Marcus hesitated a moment or two longer, and then laughed. "Well, if you say so. Drink up! Good to have you back."

David tipped back the beer, ignoring that pesky cautionary voice. He would be fine. The drink tasted as good as he remembered it. He couldn't believe he had been so foolish as to think he needed to live his life without this simple pleasure now and again.

Several hours later, with Jeanie long since in bed after having finally stopped yelling at him for his night of drinking, the pain started.

He curled up on the couch, trying to convince himself he had nothing to be concerned about. The pain would only last awhile, and then it would go away.

As he lay there he thought back to Jeanie's tirade over his evening. He didn't think he had ever seen her more upset. At the time he told her she was overreacting. He claimed that the doctor only meant to slow down, not quit altogether.

Here in the dark hours right before dawn where David's fears always surfaced the strongest, he began to realize he had made a grievous mistake—a fatal mistake.

The pain came in waves, each more devastating than the last. Within mere minutes, the torturous throbbing matched that of when Jeanie rushed him to the hospital months earlier.

He tried to stand and call the hospital. The pain barely allowed him to remain on his feet. Realization of the situation came full speed. He was dying. They'd never reach the hospital in time.

A stray memory reached his consciousness. The feeling of helplessness and evil when he'd first come back from Las Vegas. Out of any other options, David staggered to the back porch and collapsed to his knees. He could scarcely breath with the pain.

"God," he whispered, "I know I've done this to myself. I know I don't deserve your help." He doubled over in agony. "But if you take this pain away, I promise on my life that I'll never drink again."

And then the pain simply vanished. David knelt there, astonished and nearly afraid at what had happened. No trace of the pain remained. He might as well have never taken a sip of alcohol that night. Scant minutes ago he felt the icy fingers of death closing in on him and now he could sit up straight without so much as a twinge.

He couldn't believe that God had struck such a bargain with him, but David had no intentions of ever backing out on it.

"Thank you," David whispered.

Alice looked lost in contemplation. He had touched a nerve somewhere with that last batch of experiences.

"Well I've hit you with a lot today, haven't I?"

"It's not like I have anything else to do," she said. "Thank you for sharing your life story with me."

She still had so much to digest before tying it all together, David knew. He could give her a start in one area at least.

"I need to head home," he said. "But I thought I'd mention something else first. Do you remember those two friends I told you about? Chad and Marcus?"

"Yes."

"Chad's life became one continual downward spiral. He

spent his whole life drunk and miserable, never finding any peace or happiness, even in his own family. His family went down the sewer because of it. Marcus followed the same path, though to a quicker end. He committed suicide."

"How horrible," she said.

David nodded. He wished he hadn't known so many people who had ended up sharing similar fates. "The point is, I think, that the pancreatitis was one of the most physically painful experiences I've ever been through, and you now realize that says a lot. And yet I also feel it saved my life. It forced me to quit drinking."

She nodded blankly, though her mind seemed elsewhere.

"Is everything okay?"

Alice cleared her voice. "I . . . I was just wondering. And I'm almost afraid to even ask this, but what would you call your lowest low?"

She sat up straight, turning to face him. "I mean, you once told me that you've been to the farthest corner of hell and back. Where was that place? The farthest corner of hell? How could you possibly pick one part over another from a life like yours?"

For that question, David didn't have to think at all. "Las Vegas," he answered. "And not because of the city in and of itself, but what I had to go through while there."

All these years later, he still hated to think about his time in Las Vegas. He needed to answer her, however.

"Yes, I suffered a great deal as a child but I always had the faint hope that some day I would find a better way to live. As a teenager and young adult, I couldn't really see beyond the short-term. My world consisted of the present. Even when I didn't think I would live very long, I at least saw an end in sight by nature of the fact that I figured I'd be dead in a few years."

He rubbed his hands together to ward off the cold and the memory. "Las Vegas was the first time when I could stare down the long road of my life and see no happiness ahead of me for many, many years to come. I became convinced that I was destined once and for all to remain miserable. There was no hope," he added. "As you know, however, it was hitting that lowest of lows that gave me the strength to make some changes."

*Which you need to make yourself,* he wanted to add but didn't.

She sat in silence, gritting her teeth in undisguised determination. David wanted to hug her when he saw that. This was the face of a woman steadying herself for the battle ahead. He knew so. He'd seen enough of her the other way that he now recognized a spark of hope in that gaunt face.

"You'd better go home then," she said. "I think I'll stay out here for awhile."

David rose and breathed in the cold air with satisfaction. Things were finally picking up with her. He was making a difference. As he left, he made a mental note to come back as often as possible the next couple of days. He might even bring Jeanie. He knew that Jeanie had been wanting to meet Alice. Alice would be especially vulnerable once she tried to improve matters in her life and he didn't want to leave her defenseless for that crucial time period.

As he jogged back to his car through the chilly weather, David sent a silent prayer of thanks heavenward that he had finally connected with Alice.

While driving home, he stopped by a store to pick up a gift that he and Jeanie had been wanting to give to Alice. He'd meant to pick it up earlier and give it to her today, but had run out of time. *Oh well,* he thought as he tucked the gift under his arm. He would see her tomorrow.

That would be soon enough.

As a shepherd seeketh out his flock in the day that he is among his sheep that are scattered; so will I seek out my sheep, and will deliver them out of all places where they have been scattered in the cloudy and dark day.

—Ezekiel 34:12

# Chapter 16

S he checked herself out a couple days ago," the attendant said.

David stood speechless for a moment. "I don't think you heard me correctly. Alice Chambers. She stays in room 212. Age twenty-three." David's thoughts whirled. She couldn't have checked out. She wasn't ready.

"Yeah, I know who you mean. She left in a hurry too." The sleazy attendant chuckled. "Guess she'd had enough of our fine establishment."

"Did she leave any messages?"

"No."

"Do you know where she went?"

"Hey, pal, you're the one who's been hanging around her all the time. If she didn't tell you where she was going, why would she tell me? Besides, maybe she don't want to see you no more. Ever think of that?"

This made no sense. She couldn't check out. Not yet. He tucked the package he had brought under his arm and headed out the door. David had a bad feeling about this. He knew that he should have come sooner. It had been almost a week since he visited her last. Things had just kept coming up to stop him.

A week had obviously been too long. He left the building in a rush and set about trying to find her.

Where to start?

He first telephoned the other shelters. None had anybody who matched Alice's description. On a whim he stopped at the rest home to see if she had come in for a visit.

"No, we've been hoping she might stop back again," the nurse said. "Many of the residents still talk about her exquisite music."

"Thank you for your time," David answered.

David ran through her list of options. Alice didn't have family nearby. None that she'd talk to or go to for help, anyway. She didn't have any money either. Only a couple hundred dollars a month the state provided while she lived in the halfway house. That wouldn't last very far at all out on her own.

She didn't have a car, yet could have purchased a train or bus ticket to about anywhere. But where? David closed his eyes and uttered a short prayer to find her. He believed that no matter where she had gone, she was in trouble.

He felt certain after praying that she hadn't left the city. It didn't make sense for her to do so. She had nowhere to run, nor any reason to. He still couldn't guess the reason she checked out as she did, though he needed to find out why.

With only prayers guiding him, David climbed back in his car and began to comb the city. The more he thought about it, the less likely he thought that she would have traveled far at all. If she had given into despair and gave up on life, the efforts required to leave the city would be more than she would bother with.

David turned down a side street, continuing in his efforts to deduce where she could have gone.

A strong impression came to him to keep driving in the direction he was currently headed. David followed the prompting and steered his car deeper into a notoriously seedy section of neighborhood. As David delved further into the old, broken-down community, his fears deepened with regard to the trouble that might have found Alice. Most people in this neighborhood lived in dire straits. If she ended up here, she had not come to make a fresh start. A particularly shady-looking cluster of men turned their backs to him as he drove by.

Though he did not yet spot her, David decided he should park the car and go on foot. He picked up the package he had brought, locked the doors—not that it would do much good around here if someone chose to break in—and stepped out onto the street. In his day, he had spent more than his share of time in similar neighborhoods. These were the type of buildings that retained no memories, hopes, or happiness.

Alice had gone out of the frying pan and into an inferno.

A few of the people standing around cast nervous glances at him, but David paid them no attention. He very nearly walked past an alleyway when another strong impression came over him. David knew he was close. He turned into the alley and noticed a lean-to constructed of cardboard against the wall. Empty beer bottles lay scattered outside the structure.

A Bible parable came to his mind. That of the prodigal son in Luke whose life degraded to the point where he wanted nothing more than to eat the husks of the pigs he cared for. People could indeed fall that low.

He heard a rustle of movement inside the cardboard structure.

"Alice?" he asked.

Silence. He waited for a response. None came.

"Alice, if it's you in there, this is David."

"How did you find me?" she rasped. Her voice cut David deeper than ever before. It was as though he had never met her. Despair saturated her voice as thoroughly as when he had first knocked on her door.

"I did a little looking around the city. There weren't that many places to check."

She said nothing further for a moment. She must have accepted his explanation. "I'm through talking with you, David. Go away. Now."

"Alice, I think that—"

"I said *go away!*" She tore open the door of the lean-to and lurched upright, defiant. She clutched an empty bottle of whisky in one hand, holding it as a weapon. "I mean it."

Her eyes were puffy from crying, and her hair was ratted in the worst possible way. She didn't look or act inebriated at the moment, but evidence pointed that she didn't stay sober very often either.

"Alice, please—"

"You just don't get it, do you, David?" she spat the words out as an accusation. "I'm not like you. You're some kind of a . . . a superman or something. You can't be human to have survived all that you did."

She kicked down the remainder of her cardboard structure. "Look at me! Look!" She gestured the length of her body with one hand. "I'm a walking nightmare." Alice hurled the empty whisky bottle across the alleyway, shattering it against one of the brick walls. Dark green shards of glass erupted in every direction on impact.

David took a deep breath. "I know it seems that way now, but—"

"But nothing," she cut him off. "David, I'll tell you something. You really did make me think I could change and live a good life again. I'll give you that much. During your visits I started to think anything was possible. That I could be strong like you. That if you could do it, so could I."

She picked up and hurled another bottle against the wall. David sensed he should not attempt to stop her tirade. She had to ride this one through.

"Then, you want to know what happened?" She hurled another bottle. "I got scared one night. I decided to go for a walk to try and calm down. Even though I tried to fight it, I ended up walking straight to a bar to drown my fears.

"All of my supposed strength and resolve slipped away in an instant." She picked up and threw another bottle. "I don't even like drinking, but I'm weak! I can't change. Do you understand that, David? I can't change!"

Alice picked up another bottle and shrieked in anger, casting it at the wall as though attacking some ghostly version of herself. Then another. Showers of glass erupted with each throw. Alice began sobbing and yelling.

He had never seen her quite like this before, so literally on the edge. He remembered seeing many friends from his past act similarly. Shortly after they had reached this intense stage of despair, a lot of them had committed suicide.

"It's not fair!" she screamed. "Life wasn't supposed to be like this!" She dropped to the ground and buried her face in her hands, literally shaking with sobs.

*The time had come,* David thought. She needed to hear the rest of his story now, or she never would.

He brought the package in front of him and removed the brown paper. Alice never looked up as he did so. She hunkered down beside the remains of her lean-to, a woman utterly beaten by life. David honestly wondered if he had come even a day later whether she would even be alive. He prayed as mightily as he had prayed about anything that he might yet help this pour soul find herself.

"Alice, I brought something for you."

At length she uncovered her eyes and slowly looked up. Her breath caught in her throat as she studied what David held out to her. Alice was immediately and forcefully struck by the image in front of her, as David suspected she might be. She reached up and carefully grasped his simple gift, mesmerized by the picture.

A picture of the Savior.

"There is more to tell," David said softly.

There is no witness so dreadful, no accuser so terrible as the conscience that dwells in the heart of every man.

—Polybius

# Chapter 17

Alice looked at the picture of Christ, awestruck.

"There is more to tell," David repeated. "But not here."

He held his hand down to Alice and helped her stand up. "Please, this is no place for what I have to tell you next."

He walked out of the alley with Alice, who continued looking at the picture David had given her. A few people stared at them in passing but David paid them no heed. He wanted to get out of there as quickly as possible.

"Hey, Alice!" a gruff voice called. "I know you don't think you're leaving without paying us back."

David turned and saw a threatening man step from the shadows. Two other men flanked him, both of whom looked equally dangerous. All three of them approached quickly.

"Who's this? Your old man?"

Alice trembled, unable to speak.

"You owe these men money?" David asked her.

She could only nod feebly.

"How much?"

"David, no, I couldn't . . . "

"How much?" David asked again.

The men continued walking toward them.

"Three hundred dollars," she whispered.

"Listen, old man," one of them sneered when they arrived.

"I don't know what you plan on doing with Alice here, but daughter or not, she doesn't leave this neighborhood. She owes us money."

Another one chuckled. "Or trade, if we decide she's taking too long to pay us back."

The three men advanced closer. One produced a knife, his voice becoming deadly serious.

"Don't get all heroic, Pops."

David reached into an inner coat pocket and pulled out an envelope. The men eyed him first with curiosity then with excitement as they saw the contents of the envelope.

He pulled out a small portion of the bills inside and handed them over to the closest man.

"Her debt is paid. Let's go, Alice."

The men never took their eyes off the envelope as David refolded and replaced it.

"That's an awful lot of money to be carrying around a neighborhood like this," one of them said. The three men began forming a circle.

"Yeah, you should be careful," another one said. "You might get hurt."

"I think I'll be fine," David said. His confidence caught them off guard.

The leader laughed a bit nervously. "Why do you say that?"

"For one thing, the money isn't mine. It belongs to a friend."

"Well ain't that conven—"

"You see," David continued, "it's a simple question of faith. God has asked me to give this money to a friend. He'll make sure I can do so."

"Oh, a church man!" one of them exclaimed eagerly.

"Yes," David answered. "And that's why I'm not worried. He'll protect these funds one way or another."

They looked at him dangerously.

"Enough talk," the leader threatened. "Hand over the envelope or you won't make it to your car alive."

David eyed the others, a calm power settling through him. "I don't think you understand. My God has plans for these funds and they don't include you. I promise, if you try to force them from me you will regret it."

"Is that so?" one of them asked, a little uneasy.

"It's a promise," David repeated. His eyes narrowed. "One you'd better pay attention to."

He watched as the three men in front of him weighed his words. The men grew increasingly and visibly nervous. Though he carried no weapon and stood alone against them, David could tell they sensed something else at play.

There was a power present vastly greater than any these three men were familiar with.

One of them lunged forward anyway, heedless of his obvious uncertainty, only to be jerked back by the leader before he took two steps.

"We've got our money," growled the leader. "We're leaving." The three men slowly turned and walked away, leaving David and Alice alone.

"Alice, please, let's leave."

Alice stood in shock. "You could have been killed."

"No," David said. "We were protected. You'll have to believe me on that one. Now come on, this place is no good for either of us."

They finished their walk without further incident and reached David's car. Fortunately, it appeared no one had tried to break in.

"I think for your sake I should drive you away from this neighborhood, if that's okay."

Alice nodded softly.

After unlocking and opening the door for Alice, David climbed in and started the engine, grateful to have found her alive. He prayed for insight and wisdom as to how he would speak about the remainder of what he had to share with her.

To break the silence, he placed a CD in the car stereo. Piano music. David occasionally listened to classical music to soothe his nerves. He thought that perhaps piano music in particular might calm Alice down. She still seemed deeply troubled.

When the music started up, Alice closed her eyes and leaned her head against the car window, lost in thought.

Within minutes, they had left the sordid part of town he'd found her in. David wondered where he should take her.

While driving, David thought again how beautiful it was this time of year. He loved early spring possibly more than any other season. The tulips and daffodils were just barely beginning to bloom. It was a shame to miss them by staying holed up inside, or by living in Alice's most recent neighborhood. He thought it had probably been too long since Alice had cared about or even noticed anything so beautiful or simple as spring flowers.

Occasionally, Alice looked down at the picture of Christ, mesmerized by it.

David knew of a large park not far away that had a long, deep flower bed around its perimeter. Bright-colored blossoms already filled these beds. Thousands upon thousands of multi-colored tulips graced the edge of the park. He would take her there. The air was still brisk, but not so cold that she couldn't be outside.

Alice said not a word as they drove. Nor did David. He continued to gather his thoughts.

Ten minutes later they arrived at the park. "Let's take a short walk, shall we?" David suggested.

"Why do you care what happens to me, David?" Alice asked. "I still don't understand you."

"You will," he answered. "After today. I promise."

He opened the door and led her to a wooden bench overlooking the sea of flowers. She scarcely seemed to notice them as they sat down. She carried the picture he had brought her, yet didn't look at it very often either. She essentially stared off at the horizon, looking at everything and nothing simultaneously.

David took a deep breath. It was time.

"You know what religion I belong to, don't you?"

"Mormon. Like my Aunt Amelia." Alice cleared her throat.

"She's tried telling me about it, but I've never been very interested." She risked a quick glance to David. "I'm afraid that's still the case."

David merely nodded. He had expected that response. "I understand. But you need to know why I survived what I did. The full name of the Church is the Church of Jesus Christ of Latter Day Saints." He emphasized the words "Jesus Christ."

She said nothing in response.

"You said only an hour ago that you think I'm some sort of walking miracle. You told me you can't believe why I'm not crazy or dead."

"I can't," she repeated. "And you *are* a walking miracle. You're stronger than I could ever hope to be."

"That is where you're wrong. I'm actually rather weak."

For a few moments Alice remained silent and still. Then she looked at David with genuine exasperation. "You can't possibly believe that."

"Alice, you see only who stands before you today. You know enough of my past to realize that I was lost. Broken. I could scarcely control my own actions. If somebody threatened me, I became a raging maniac. I drank too much. Partied too often. A strong man, truly strong, would not have done those things."

"David, you can't blame yourself for the way you were raised. How else could you have reacted? The point I'm making is that it didn't kill you. You eventually overcame it. That is the difference between you and me."

"No, the only real difference between us is that you don't yet know the man in that picture," David said. "You need to understand something, Alice. We're all weak. We all make mistakes. I've made more than my share, in fact. But we were never expected to try and go through this life alone or on our own merits. He is there to help us. All we have to do is ask."

"I wish I could believe that."

They sat quietly, each juggling thoughts.

At length, Alice continued. "I look at this picture and see a dream. It's a pleasant dream, mind you, but still just a dream. I can understand why so many people choose to believe in it." She brushed aside a length of her hair and took a deep breath.

She continued. "It must be comforting to believe that somebody above always watches over you. But David, how could there possibly be a God? If there was one, how could he possibly be said to love us?"

"He does."

"I'm sorry, David, but I truly can't believe that. I am sincerely glad that you have found peace and happiness in your church, but I personally can't believe a God would let someone go through things like you have. I know I certainly haven't felt anyone watching over me. Or Lily."

She placed a hand on his shoulder. "But thank you for the picture."

It was as though a stifling, thick curtain were being wrapped around her slender frame time and time again, David thought. She was already building up her defenses against life and hope. This wasn't about religion, it was about giving into despair. He wasn't about to let that happen again.

"After I joined the Church," David said, "I experienced a whole new level of suffering."

She jolted upright as though she'd been stung. He doubted anything he'd ever said to her had surprised her quite so much.

"What?" Her tone was saturated with incredulity.

David wished there had been perhaps a more tactful way to state things, but Alice had never responded to subtlety. And after all, there was really no better way to put it.

"Alice, whether you want to realize it or not, there is a war being fought over each and every one of us. A very real war. You will recall that I had decided after Las Vegas to change my life. It didn't take me much longer to meet and marry Jeanie, as you know. About a year after our marriage, I found and embraced the gospel.

"But in this war, when you start making correct choices, the opposing side pulls out all the stops to try and get you back."

✦ ✦ ✦

Even though he knew this was where he was supposed to be, David could scarcely breath. He wanted to run screaming from this building or throw himself off a cliff in an effort to stop the torturous feelings inside.

Simply coming to church at all today had been a complete battle, as it had the entire three months since he started attending church. It felt like demons had climbed on his back and dug their claws into his flesh with unabated resolve. It had taken every bit of his resolve merely to show up.

Now that he had arrived, he felt absolutely no better. Worse, perhaps, if it were possible.

The man at the pulpit spoke on immorality. David's whole body tensed with the anxiety and guilt that each word brought him.

Jeanie sensed his concerns and placed a reassuring hand on his arm. David could scarcely feel her touch. He could hardly see, feel, or hear anything beyond the consuming thoughts of hell and fire that drowned out everything else.

Maybe he had been wrong in thinking he could change, David began to realize. He made some decisions several months ago to try and correct his life, but he might be too late in life to turn around. God obviously didn't want anything to do with him.

The missionaries told David about the Spirit. They said it brought peace. Comfort. The tumultuous feelings thrashing around within him and the literal wrenching in his gut could be described as anything but peaceful. He felt as though God himself were scowling down on him, reminding him in absolute detail of all the horrific things he had done in his life.

The man at the pulpit continued to speak on the dire nature of immorality. How God took it so seriously. This man could just as easily have been referring to lying, stealing, the sins of drinking. Giving into anger. Invariably, every single time David had come to church he had felt lower and lower. He began to realize the full extent of his guilt and shame.

Surely God could not love him after all he had done. Even though he remembered hearing in class the other week that church is a 'hospital for sinners and not a health club for saints' David could no longer think he was included in that group. There were sinners, and then there were lost souls. David was surely the latter.

But he had promised God he would try. If it killed him, David was going to continue coming to church. He could never make up for what he had done, he knew, and of course he would never find full favor with God again. It was too late to hope that he would be included in the upper kingdoms of heaven, but David would do his best not to land smack dab in the middle of hell.

Obviously God didn't yet want anything to do with David. He still knew that God loved him, as he always had, but David also knew that God was more than a little displeased with how he had wasted his life so far. If it killed him, and David thought that was a very real possibility, he would still come to try and better his life. He was thoroughly beyond any serious or lasting repair, though he wanted to get as close as possible to someone the Lord would be proud of.

The guilt washed over him once more as the speaker quoted additional scriptures on the dire nature of immoral sin—how it's right up there with murder and other grievous offenses.

David wished for a moment that the man would dwell a bit longer on murder. At least there was one safe haven that David wouldn't have to feel guilty about. Maybe the only one.

As the meeting dragged on, David's back literally tightened so completely he heard it pop several times. His whole body tensed from the sheer power of emotions and regrets coursing through him. This was similar to how he had felt as a child, testifying in front of his schoolmates. He felt exposed, as though the whole room could look at him and see a vile sinner in a righteous man's clothing. God could certainly see it, so why not them?

The irony of what the man said next struck David forcefully. At the great day of the Lord, there would be some who would gladly hide under a mountain if they could. *How perfect a solution,* David thought. A mountain. He would gladly hide under a mountain right then and there, to say nothing of the great day of the Lord. He would do whatever might keep his unworthy existence from the penetrating eyes of God. However, he knew not even a mountain could ever hide him sufficiently.

No matter where he went, under a mountain or at the bottom of the ocean, God would still see with a perfect eye the child who had so completely disappointed and shamed him.

Tears slid painfully down David's cheek as the speaker continued.

Cast all your cares on God; that anchor holds.

—Alfred Lord Tennyson

# Chapter 18

"Get a grip," David told himself in the mirror. He stared at his reflection, trembling from the after effects of the incessant vomiting he'd done for the last half hour. After a little over a year of regular church attendance, the weekly ritual wasn't getting any easier for David.

He clutched the sink for support. The man wearing a suit and tie who looked back at him from the mirror was haggard at best. David chastised himself. All of this anxiety over a few simple responsibilities at church. Couldn't he shrug them off?

Except it was much more than conducting meetings that tormented him. While standing in front of much more qualified people did fill him with an unmistakable sense of dread, the anxiety within him had much deeper roots. After a full year of going to church, his guilt and shame in front of God had not improved in the least.

If anything, it had grown worse by the week. It was as though the harder he tried, the angrier God became. For a full year, David had wrestled with demons simply to make it some place he thought he belonged. Now he was beginning to wonder why he bothered. He questioned whether he had spent all this time trying to force something that would never fit. Perhaps God really didn't want him there after all.

The continued stresses of providing for his young family only added to the burden. He'd started his roofing business, which was not doing well at all. Any month now, things could fold under and David would lose the house, the car—everything. He prayed for success and help, though he had difficulty expecting that the Lord would help him. It wasn't that God didn't care about him, David knew, but he certainly hadn't earned any favors from God. That would be expecting too much.

Month by month, his willpower had been slipping. It seemed that no matter how low he fell, there were always new depths to slide into the following week.

There had been a time when he knew how to laugh. No longer. Once he had felt optimistic about his future. Now his business seemed doomed to fail. Once he had believed that because God loved him, David could expect help from him. Lately he wondered if God had become so disappointed that he had turned his back.

If David had to put the whole experience into words, he would say that each and every one of his virtues were being stripped away from him, one at a time.

Though living had never been easy for David, this was the first time he feared that life after death would not be an improvement. He suspected that somehow he had already failed the test in life. How else could he feel so hollow?

Someone tried the handle on the other side of the bathroom door and found it locked. David couldn't bring himself to leave quite yet. Retreating footsteps indicated the person outside had opted to find another facility. David felt relieved; he didn't know how long he'd take to compose himself.

Why his Church leaders bothered to give him assignments he couldn't guess. Maybe they thought it would help him grow and he would eventually do a good job. But they were wrong. He was more than simply inadequate. He had hardly anything to offer. He wanted desperately to experience the Savior's love that so many others in the Church talked about, but that too remained out of reach.

Maybe in his childhood he had felt that love, but no more.

He wanted to develop kindness and charity inside and yet he realized all too well that he'd become nothing more than a shell of whom he once hoped to be.

All his strength had left him. He remained nothing beyond a mere shadow of his old self. Going through the motions wore extremely thin. If not for the sheer willpower and work ethic forced into him since early childhood, he would have quit long ago. That was the only thing carrying him forward anyway. Willpower. No matter the determination, however, a man trying to open a locked door still makes no progress.

The way was barred for him. David had come to accept that fact in the past little while. He still believed the Church to be true, and still believed he needed to do all he could to restore his life, but he could never measure up.

He flushed the toilet and stood, adjusting his tie in the mirror. Soon he would have to wear the face others expected. Smiling, care-free. And then he'd go into the meetings and stand before everybody, displaying his faults for all in the room to see.

Another gripping stab of anxiety twisted his gut mercilessly. David pitched forward and dry-heaved into the toilet once more, trying to block out the mental image of those faces that would scrutinize him later that day. The faces of people who didn't have such devastating pasts. People who had cause to hope, and who could go to sleep at night without bawling until their eyes nearly swelled shut. People who lived simple lives of contentedness and satisfaction. Lives without fear and constant, tormenting guilt.

David's gut churned as the images flashed by.

"Please help me," David pleaded in prayer. "Help me to get through the day. It's all I ask."

Emotional turmoil ripped into David's heart yet again as he remembered his many sins as he often did while praying. Another floodgate of tears rushed to the surface. His whole body convulsed with an immensity of anguish that cloaked him like a thick, dark blanket.

*What could God possibly want from such a troubled soul?* David wondered. He yearned so badly to change and find happiness, but it remained forever out of reach. Happiness, real happiness, sounded like a distant and laughable dream. He had to content himself in seeking mere survival, which was fast beginning to seem unattainable as well.

With another violent bout of stress-laden anxiety, David retched until he thought his head would explode.

Alice seemed deeply perplexed. "That's not at all what I expected to hear," she said.

David nodded. He understood her confusion. "For that first year, I really believed I would die. Living became so painful that I could barely stand to wake up."

For several long moments, Alice and David sat together in silence. Alice reached down and plucked a single red tulip, caressing it as a mother would her child.

"Then what happened?" She didn't look up from examining her flower.

"What I'm about to tell you is so very personal that I can't share it in its entirety," David said. "But you need to know at least some of this experience if any of what I've shared with you so far is to make any sense."

Finally Alice looked up, a quiet eagerness evident on her face to hear what came next.

David collected his thoughts. "Shortly after the time I just told you about, a little over a year after joining the Church, I had a dream."

Alice nodded her encouragement for him to continue.

"In the dream, I saw myself as a young child thrashing and sputtering in the canal directly in front of my house. Though as a child I knew how to swim, in this dream I could barely keep my head above water. The water whipped me along with force and speed that I couldn't fight. Ina stood there watching, along with her grandchildren and Karl. They all stood mere feet away and laughed at me while I flailed in the water.

They kept pointing and mocking me as I drowned."

David blinked his eyes to see past the forming tears. "Make no mistake, Alice, I truly was drowning in my dream. And never before had a dream felt more real than this one. It was so real I could taste the water.

"Some fifty yards from the house lay a deep culvert under the road. This particular culvert ran underground for at least fifty yards. As kids we stayed far, far away from it. If the swift water pulled you under, you'd die for sure before reemerging at the other end. In my dream, the water mercilessly pushed me toward the fatal culvert. I screamed for help whenever I could clear my mouth of water long enough. I knew I was going to die. I had no doubt about it. Unless one of them would help me, and none moved to do so, my life would be over. I had scant seconds left to live and needed somebody—anybody—to pull me to safety. Yet no one would."

Alice's lower lip trembled as her own eyes teared up.

"My time had run out. With a sickening acceptance of the inevitable, I stared in horror at the last length of open sky I would ever see alive. The end had come."

David cleared his voice of the constricting emotions. "And then, exactly as I was being sucked under, a powerful arm clothed in white reached down and snatched me out of the water. The stranger pulled me to safety. With a heart bursting in gratitude I looked up and wanted to stammer my thanks to whoever had rescued me.

"I found myself looking into the eyes and face of the man in that picture," David said softly, gesturing to the picture of Christ. "The Savior. I could tell you the color of his eyes, the color of his hair. He looked on me with such love that I wanted to never leave."

Tears slid down David's face as he relived the memory. "He pulled me close, crushing me in an embrace. Then he spoke to me, Alice. He said . . . he said I didn't have to hurt any more. He told me that he loved me. For the first time in my life, I felt that perfect love I had sought for so long. The pure love of

Christ was not simply mine to touch, I was filled by it."

Alice began to cry as well.

Emotion laced David's words. "That is all I can tell you of that dream, but you need to know something. The Lord loves you just as much."

Insight flooded into David as Alice began crying harder. Her soul was opened wide for him to see inside. Her carefully structured defenses disintegrated before his eyes as intuition born not from himself carried thoughts and messages deep inside. He knew exactly what to say next.

"Whatever mistakes you might have made, He still loves you. That I promise you." She broke down at those words, sobbing so violently she could scarcely breath. "You are nowhere near so far gone that you can't find happiness again. You are not unworthy of His love. You are a good person. The Lord knows it and He's making sure I do as well."

She couldn't speak; she had become so consumed by outletting her grief.

"I think I finally understand exactly why I had to tell you so vividly about my life," David said. "You needed to realize not only how thoroughly broken I had become, but how far I fell because of it. And how difficult the path back was. The road back is anything but easy, and we make many mistakes."

He leaned in. "But that's the whole point, Alice. I was dead in the water without the Savior. I had nothing left to give. I was swept along by the evil forces of this world and for all my struggling I couldn't save myself."

Placing a hand on her shoulder, he continued. "And neither can you. Alice, you're not strong enough to do this on your own. You need his help. We all do."

Alice continued to weep.

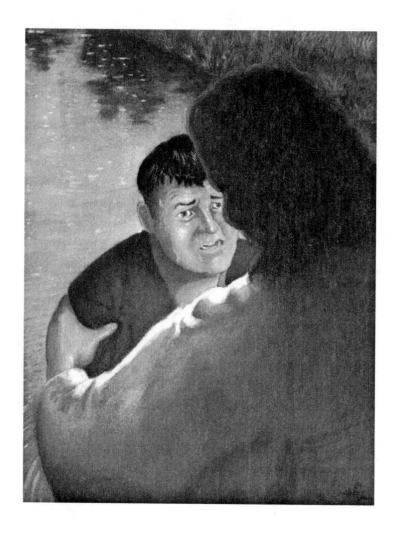

Therefore may God grant unto you, my brethren, that ye may begin to exercise your faith unto repentance, that ye begin to call upon his holy name, that he would have mercy upon you; Yea, cry unto him for mercy; for he is mighty to save.

—Alma 34: 17–18

# Chapter 19

For a few minutes, David said nothing as Alice continued to cry.

"My time with you is about up," David finally said when she calmed down enough.

"You've heard just about everything I need to tell you. But first, I need to show you something." David pulled out his wallet and flipped it open to a picture of himself and Jeanie.

"This was taken on our twenty-second wedding anniversary. We went to Cancun to celebrate—a place we have visited many times together. We love it there."

Alice dabbed at her eyes long enough to glance at the picture. David flipped through picture after picture in his wallet.

"And these are our children. Some from our first marriages, others from our marriage together. And here are some pictures of our grandkids. Cutest little kids you'd ever want to meet."

She smiled at seeing the photo of his granddaughter's first birthday, her face covered in chocolate cake.

"Alice, don't give up! So much good has happened to me since I finally turned my life around. It wasn't an easy road at all. In fact, it took several years before I stopped throwing up over anxiety about church assignments. The road is long and challenging, but worth it!

"As I look back now, I see how truly blessed I have been

over the years. My family is strong, my business successful, and I know that the Lord loves me. I have hope, and have had for some time now, that I can meet my Savior with a clear conscience. That I will be received with loving arms when I pass on."

Tears continued to fall down Alice's cheeks. "I don't know how to do all of this."

"Just a moment," David said. He returned to his car and retrieved a small package he had been waiting until the right time to give her. That time had come.

"This is for you," he said. She unwrapped it. It was a Book of Mormon.

"I've never read scriptures before," she whispered. "I don't think I ever even prayed before."

"Alice, this is not the time and place for me to try and explain this sacred book to you in any detail. I hope the day comes soon that you will look into it. This book can place you on a path that will save your life. I do, however, need to share a few pieces of my testimony with you Alice. Things you need to hear.

"First, your daughter Lily is alive. I know that as sure as I know you sit in front of me."

A desperate flash of hope crossed Alice's face.

"I also know that you will see her again. If you follow the path this book places you on, the path to Christ, you can live with her again after this life and raise her as your child."

"That's not possible." Alice said, afraid to believe the words.

"Yes, it is. I can't make you believe that, but you can find out for yourself. I repeat, you can be with Lily again. Also, it is possible for you to find love and happiness in this life. Real love. Real happiness. You can fall in love with a good man and be married to him, not until death do you part, but for all eternity. You can start a family again.

"You can know exactly why you are here on this earth, and what you need to do to find happiness. You can have the constant companionship of the Holy Ghost to guide you in all you do. It is possible to be so exquisitely full of joy that you literally cannot feel despair. Just as the Savior snatched me out of that culvert, he can rescue you."

He took her hand in his own and might as well have been a father to his wayward daughter.

"The only thing I ask of you, Alice, is that you give the Lord a chance to work in you and change your life. Seek his help. You have so much to give, so much ahead of you. You're only twenty-three years old. Though you can't conceive of it now, it is possible that in short order your life could be amazingly meaningful. Not necessarily easy, but full of purpose."

"I will consider your words," Alice said. "But everything you're telling me sounds impossible."

"Nothing is impossible."

David reached down and clutched her to him as she wept on his shoulder for several more minutes. He could feel her grief melting away. A warmth spread within him, the intensity of which he had only felt a few times before. He had said all he needed to.

She finally finished crying and pushed back, bleary eyed.

"And that's what I've come to tell you," he said. "But there is one more thing."

He reached in his pocket and pulled out the envelope. As soon as she saw it, she recoiled in protest.

"David, no! You can't!"

But he was already holding it out to her. "This doesn't belong to me."

She shoved it back at him. "No, David! I can't take it. I won't. You've done so much for me already. I'll be all right."

For the moment, David set the envelope down on the bench. It seemed to take her edge away. She wasn't all up in arms for the moment.

"Let me tell you a little something about miracles, Alice. Several times early on in the Church I needed the Lord's help in very real ways.

"There was one time about two years after I joined the

Church when my roofing business had torn the roof off of an apartment building."

She was appropriately sidetracked from the envelope, David realized. *Good.*

"One thing you need to understand about my line of work is that you never tear off roofs until you've checked and rechecked the weather. Rain in an open building can cause more structural damage than you can imagine. And whereas I was especially new and financially vulnerable, one mistake like that would have ruined me for good. I'd have had to go into shoveling cow poop for a living, or something like that."

He laughed good naturedly. She didn't respond likewise.

Boy, that envelope had raised a few of her hackles, he noticed. She didn't want to let her guard down just yet. She kept glancing at the envelope like it was a snake, coiled to strike. For the time being, he pulled the envelope closer to him. She relaxed a small measure; however, not fully.

*Close enough,* he figured.

"Well, this particular apartment building was very pricey. And we had the roof ripped completely off, as I said. Normally we tear off the roofs and replace them the same day. But as it turns out, this one ended up needing new plywood so we had to leave it for the next day."

Alice had the look of a woman who knew she was getting lured into something she didn't want, but had no way of pinning it down. She continued to listen suspiciously and silently.

"Out of nowhere, this freak rainstorm came in, totally against the weather reports. We're talking the mother of all rainstorms. Clouds so black you could hardly see the sunlight behind them."

He finally repocketed the envelope. She wouldn't stop glancing down at it until it was safely out of view. Only then did she really relax.

"Now a couple of weeks earlier, Alice, I had been to a church meeting. One of our Church leaders, an apostle named Elder Boyd K. Packer, had left a blessing on us. He told us that we would have the ministering of angels, should we call upon them. Now that's something we all have anyway," he explained, "but when the blessing comes from an apostle, it's that much more sacred and special."

"So his words came to me that night as I watched the clouds roll in. There was no way I could possibly cover up the building in time. I went out on the back porch and looked to the heavens. 'Lord,' I said, 'Elder Packer promised us ministering angels if we need them. And I need them. I need them to protect that building.'"

"What happened?" Alice asked, transfixed.

David almost smiled. She had already forgotten the envelope.

"No sooner did I say those words than the most wonderful, spiritual, peaceful feeling came over me. I knew instantly and without doubt that everything would be fine."

"Even with all that rain?"

"Yes. I felt so completely reassured that I simply went back into the house and forgot about the building. I had the promise of the Lord that it would be taken care of. Minutes later, my foreman calls in a panic. I told him not to worry about it, that things would be fine."

"And did he listen to you?"

David laughed. "Oh no. He went down that night to try and cover it up anyway. The next morning we drove in and looked at the building together. The foreman finally just hunched his shoulders. 'I don't get it,' he had said. 'Water was pouring so hard on an identical building five feet away that water rushed over the gutters. It rained and rained and rained everywhere but on our building.'"

"Are you serious?" Alice asked.

"Yes. Not a drop fell in our apartment building. Not a drop." He emphasized the words to drive home the point. "You see, I knew I had to trust the Lord. Plastic would never have helped in time. The Lord promised me the building would be fine. He kept his promise."

David smiled. "That's always the way. If God wants us to do something, he always provides a way. So, when last week he told me that you would need some money—"

The walls were back up in a flash. "David!"

"Now, hold on. Let me finish." She looked ready to grind him into powder. For the life of him, David couldn't say why he found it amusing. He just about laughed out loud at her fiercely stubborn countenance.

"When I realized that you would need some money to change your life—really change it—I sat down and tried to figure out how much. With the Lord's help, I came up with a figure."

"David, I saw what was in that envelope and I don't think—"

"Alice, were you ever on the debate team in school?"

The question caught her off guard. "What? No, why do you ask?"

"Mostly out of curiosity. So as I was saying, I came up with a figure." He held up a finger to silence her next rebuttal. Miraculously, she held her tongue. "So, once I realized how much you required, I simply knelt down and told the Lord I needed that amount.

"Being your own boss is a funny thing," he blurted out, sidetracking her further before she could protest. She looked thoroughly perplexed at his change of tactics. David was enjoying himself immensely.

"It's great to be your own boss, Alice. You get to set your own hours. Take vacations when you want. Have control over your working conditions."

"David, I don't see how—"

"But it also has plenty of downsides," he interrupted. Wow, was she tough to talk to, all worked up like this. Her spunk made him want to smile and hug her again. She reminded him more than ever of one of his daughters.

"Collections is one of those downsides," he continued. "In roofing, you can't receive all the pay up front. We get a lot of our money only after the job is done. And, unfortunately for me, sometimes the customer doesn't want to pay.

"One such job awhile back went sour. We finished the job and he didn't give us our money. We tried and tried, sent him to collections, but he still never paid. With this job, as with more others than I'd like to admit, we had to chalk it up as a write-off. A no-pay."

Alice squirmed in her seat, probably sensing where this was headed.

"So on the very same day I told the Lord how much money I needed for you, I'm driving along in my truck. Jeanie calls me on the cell phone and says, 'You're not gonna believe this, but that job from so long ago just sent you a check.' Alice, it was for the same amount—the exact amount—I had asked the Lord for. Not the amount of this customer's bill, he still owes us some, but every dollar he sent was a dollar more than I expected to get from him.

"These funds belong to you," David said. "The Lord made that clear enough. I'm not sure how they are to help you, but you'll find out. It's not so much as you think, either. Just enough to get you on your feet. A few months to live on, if you're careful."

"David, I'm sorry, but I just can't."

"Well I'm sorry too, because you don't have a lot of choice here," David said. He took the envelope out of his pocket and set it between them on the bench.

"There. I'll never touch that envelope again! I feel so much better." He grinned at a thoroughly flustered Alice.

"It will just blow away then," Alice responded, "because I'm not going to pick it up either."

"Fine by me." David stretched his arm muscles high above his head. "At least it's now out my hands. And I've gotta tell you, I feel a lot better."

"David!"

A gust of wind picked up the envelope and carried it ten feet where it landed in the flowers. Alice shot him a look of pure frustration.

"David, come on. You can't just let it blow away!"

"I'm not the one letting it blow away. That would be you."

The breeze picked it up again, carrying it another twenty feet. Alice looked ready to scream. David locked his hands behind his head, stretched his feet out, and whistled.

"Beautiful day, isn't it?" he said.

Another gust of wind slipped through the trees, grabbing the envelope a third time. Alice finally set her picture and Book of Mormon down on the bench in a huff.

"You are impossible!" she blurted out.

She ran off to chase the escaping envelope and David had to laugh out loud at her plight. To his great astonishment, Alice joined in with him. The envelope danced and skittered around the park, with her chasing it as a little girl would a butterfly. All the while, she laughed long and clear.

David felt a lightness of spirit at hearing her. In all the times he'd met Alice, he never expected to hear such pure laughter from her.

Eventually, the unruly envelope became tangled in a rose bush and Alice snatched it victoriously, holding it aloft like a football at a touchdown. David clapped at the performance.

"Bravo!" he called out.

Alice performed an impromptu little bow, and then scurried back with her prize in hand.

"Are you sure piano was the best way to go?" he asked. "You'd have made a fine soccer player."

She laughed again and, to his great relief, actually pocketed the envelope. She then turned quite serious.

"David, I don't know what to say. Nobody has been so kind to me before. Ever."

"Alice, we're all here to help each other. I've been helped financially, emotionally, and spiritually, at many different times in my life. This is all part of the Lord's plan. I just hope you can find the strength to try and turn your life around."

She took a deep breath. "I think I can promise you that much at least. I will try. Whether or not I'll succeed I can't say, but I want to see what else may be out there for me. As for your or any religion," she paused, seeking for the right words. "I don't really know. I will read your book, though I make no promises beyond that."

David smiled. That was plenty.

"Fair enough. Now, Alice, where would you like me to take you?"

She closed her eyes in thought, gathering courage. "The airport," she decided.

That made perfect sense, David thought. A fresh start away from all the memories and demons from her past.

"Where will you go?" he asked.

She shook her head. "I don't know. But I think I'll be able to figure it out once I'm there."

David admired her courage. Not many people would have the guts to completely relocate on the spur of the moment.

Alice picked up her picture and Book of Mormon and walked toward the car.

"Ready when you are," she said. She sounded a lot more nervous than she was trying to act.

After letting her in, David walked around to his side of the car and climbed behind the steering wheel. For the second time that day, he turned on the piano music and they traveled in silence. Funny, with as much as he and Alice had spoken over the past few weeks that silence seemed the most appropriate.

As David glanced periodically over at Alice in the passenger seat, his heart went out to her. She looked increasingly more anxious as the miles rolled by. He was reminded of his own children as they left for college and other venues. The anxiety of the unknown was scary to almost everyone. Her bravery truly impressed him. He'd half expected her to stay around in her familiar environment for a few days while trying to formulate a game plan.

Yet as he considered it, this was really the best thing she could do. Get a clean break from everything before she had a chance to talk herself out of it. Find something new before her old acquaintances caught up with her.

By the time he pulled up to the airport, it seemed that a lot of her resolve had slipped, however. She still appeared determined enough to go through with it, but a pretty significant amount of fear was evident on her face.

"You might consider Hawaii," David said. The thought had come from nowhere.

The suggestion made Alice laugh sarcastically. "You're kidding, right?"

"No, I'm serious. I've been there a couple of times down through the years. Beautiful place. And you wouldn't have any problem finding work. Especially in the summer. If nothing else, they're always looking for help in the pineapple fields. Do you like pineapple?"

Alice laughed again, this time in anticipation. "I love it."

She bit her lip in excitement.

"Do you really think I could find a job there? I wouldn't end up in the gutter?" Her enthusiasm at the prospect of going to Hawaii was palpable. She reminded David of a little girl who'd just received a long-awaited bicycle as a gift.

"Well, you're chances of finding work there are as good or better than about anywhere else I can think of. Very touristy this time of year. They need lots of seasonal help. And besides, if you do end up in the gutter, at least it would be a Hawaiian gutter."

She smiled broadly. "Hawaii," she said, trying the word out for size.

David could tell by the electricity on her face that her destination was a foregone conclusion whether she realized it yet or not. It would be perfect for her.

She lunged forward and gave David another hug.

"You're the sweetest man I've ever known. You're the father I've never had." She gave him a quick kiss on the cheek—a daughter kissing her dad goodbye—and scooped up the picture and book he gave her.

"I'd better leave before I lose my nerve to go through with this. Goodbye, David, and thank you for everything."

"Aloha," he said. She scrunched up her face. "In Hawaii, that means both hello and goodbye. Just in case you end up there and all."

"Aloha then," Alice replied. She opened the door and walked briskly to the airport front door.

He couldn't believe her transformation from only earlier that day. It seemed nearly impossible that a person could travel such a broad emotional spectrum in the space of one day. That same morning she had crawled out of her cardboard lean-to looking more dead than alive. Now she looked like a child underneath a Christmas tree.

She turned and waved one last time, grinning, before slipping inside the airport.

A tremendous feeling of calm settled over David as he watched her go. He had done everything he needed to. He knew so. The rest was in God's hands.

As he drove away from the airport, he tried to imagine what the shores of Hawaii would look like to someone who had lived in both literal and figurative shadows for most of her life.

Wherefore, whoso believeth in God might with surety hope for a better world, yea, even a place at the right hand of God, which hope cometh of faith, maketh an anchor to the souls of men, which would make them sure and steadfast, always abounding in good works, being led to glorify God.

—Ether 12: 4

# Chapter 20

David thought often of Alice over those first few months. He and his wife discussed her many times, wondering if she ever found any joy in life. Though Jeanie had never met her, she had come to think of Alice as a daughter, as had David. More than once, they had nearly hopped on a plane bound for Hawaii to see if they could find her. But after that first summer had come and passed, they figured she would be some place else and stopped thinking about making the trip. Now that a little over two years had slipped by, they felt certain she was long gone.

Shortly after David dropped Alice off at the airport, her aunt Amelia had also moved. When last he spoke with Amelia, she hadn't heard from Alice either.

He visited and helped many people in his capacity as bishop, but something about Alice stuck with him for a long time. She was so lost when he first met her. So completely full of anguish. Maybe he connected with her in such a strong manner because he could relate with her background. Jeanie thought as much.

If he had a means to contact her, he would do so. He wanted to know many things about her. Had she found happiness? Love? Hawaii? For all he knew, she could have had second thoughts in the terminal and caught a taxi back into town.

Except he didn't like to think that. He liked to think that she had a great summer in paradise and put her life back together.

Eventually, the busy nature of his own life pushed thoughts of Alice from his mind after a year or so. He and Jeanie had their hands full with children and grandchildren. His duties as bishop were time-consuming as always, and his roofing business stayed busier than ever. By the end of the second year, he had almost forgotten Alice. Neither he nor Jeanie brought her up any more.

And so when a knock sounded at his front door and he answered, he couldn't understand for the life of him why this beautiful young lady on the porch grinned up at him like he was her favorite uncle.

"David!" the young lady screamed, and in a flash covered the distance to crush him in a bear hug.

Few things in life truly surprised David. He could roll with a lot of uncertainties and had learned to expect the unexpected. But not for a million dollars could he find an explanation for this stranger who seemed determined to cut off his circulation in a single, never ending vice grip of a hug.

Had he developed a trace of amnesia? This young woman obviously thought she knew him.

"I can't believe it's really you," the young woman said.

At length he broke away from the hug. She looked up at him, obviously expecting some form of recognition. Her obvious anticipation tortured David. As soon as he would open his mouth and reveal his memory lapse, he would undoubtedly insult this visitor horribly. He hated when he couldn't remember a person's name, but to completely forget their existence was something else entirely.

Still, he had no defense. It had to be done. "I'm so sorry . . . how do I know you?"

The young woman blinked, plainly surprised beyond measure at the question. After a few moments, however, she started laughing. Something about her laugh sounded familiar to David, though he couldn't place it. The young woman's face lit up like a Christmas tree when she smiled. Where had he seen that before?

Jeanie came down from the stairs, cheerful and curious at the same time. "David, who's at the door?"

Before David could answer, the young stranger addressed Jeanie.

"I think your husband's gone a little brain dead in the last couple of years. Or maybe he just saves lives so often he can't keep track of them all. You must be Jeanie."

The young lady walked all the way into the house as though she owned the place and hugged Jeanie for all she was worth.

Last couple of years. Saved lives. David's mind spun, trying to piece it all together. That laugh. That smile.

It couldn't be.

"Alice?"

Alice barely had time to nod her head before Jeanie screamed and practically snapped Alice's back in a second, much more enthusiastic hug. David could scarcely believe what his eyes were registering.

This wasn't the Alice he had met two years ago, not by a long shot. Her hair was shorter now, for one, but that only began to describe her transformation. She now had a deep, vibrant tan whereas the Alice he remembered was pale and sickly looking. This woman possessed an athletic, robust physique. The Alice he recalled had appeared emaciated, gaunt, and hollow-cheeked.

The Alice from two years ago had sorrow etched deeply into her face. This young lady positively glowed with happiness. She had smile creases where frown lines used to be. Though only twenty-three years old when he first met her, she had looked much older then.

Now, two years later, she looked ten years younger than before. The whole transformation had a rather dizzying effect on David. But for the auburn color of her hair, the resplendent young woman in front of him looked nothing whatsoever like the Alice he recalled. Cosmetic surgery could not have made her appear any less like her old self. The difference was more drastic than he would have thought possible.

"Jeanie," David said, "I'd like you to meet Alice Chambers."

Alice laughed. "Oh, so you do remember me?" she said, teasing a bit.

David scratched his head. "Well of course I do. You just don't look anything like I remember."

"Two years in Hawaii will do that to you," she said.

"So you did go! And you've lived there this whole time?" He thrilled upon learning she not only made it to those sun-drenched islands in the Pacific, she had obviously liked it enough to stay long-term.

"Yes, and I have something very important to give you," she answered. "Here, I've been dying to do this for months!"

She handed a small envelope to David. He opened it as a very nervous yet excited Alice stood by. Inside he found two plane tickets to Hawaii, in three months time.

"Please say you can go!" she pleaded. "You have to!"

His mind tumbled around as he examined the tickets. Why would she want he and Jeanie to go to Hawaii?

"Alice, what's going on?"

She grinned again and handed him a second, larger envelope. He and Jeanie shared a knowing glance. These particular envelopes usually betrayed their contents before they were even opened.

He broke the seal on the second envelope and pulled out a wedding invitation. Alice and a very good-looking young man smiled at the camera, every inch in love from what the picture revealed.

"You're getting married! That's fantastic."

"Yes, but look where."

He scanned the announcement and nearly fell over.

"In . . . in the Hawaii *temple*?"

She nodded again, tears falling down her cheeks. David and Jeanie both began to cry as well once the full realization set in.

"David," Alice said. "I had to deliver these in person. There hasn't been a day in my life these past two years that I haven't drawn on the strength you gave me from your kindness on my behalf. You literally saved my life. You taught me all I needed to know to find happiness."

David wanted to respond but his heart was too full. Words couldn't come out.

"I waited until now to contact you in any way because I wanted to work through everything first before I saw you next. My own test and reward system. When things got tough, I just imagined the thrill of standing before you today and personally inviting you to my wedding. You've inspired me more than you could possibly know."

Alice clasped her hands. "I've got quite a lot to tell you, you know."

For the next several hours she spoke almost nonstop to David and Jeanie about her life in Hawaii. She had found work almost immediately when she first arrived, which proved fortunate because the plane fare chewed up a big chunk of the money. The funds ran out exactly as her first paycheck came in. True to David's calculating, he had given her precisely what she needed.

Hawaii was a balm to her soul. Simply being there lifted years of burden. She kept her promise to David and started reading the Book of Mormon. With all the hustle and bustle of fitting into a new home and lifestyle, it had taken her a full year to complete it.

At the end of the year she found the promise at the back of the book and decided to ask God if it were true. When she received her confirmation, she surprised the first set of missionaries she came across—not hard to do in Hawaii, she said with a bit of feigned scolding to David for suggesting she go there—by asking how she went about getting baptized.

Her life became gloriously happy, if also extremely difficult at times. She too had had a long, uphill battle feeling worthy of the blessings of the Lord. The loss of Lily sometimes left her forlorn and empty, but she continued forward.

While in Hawaii she tried contacting her parents for the first time in five years. She took the news that her mother had died from throat cancer a year and a half earlier pretty hard. After her mother died, her father fell into some serious trouble with the law and disappeared from the authorities. For months she attempted to track him down, to no avail.

Though her relationship with her parents had never been good, it hurt to have them gone forever so suddenly. She continued to hope that she might find her father some day, though from what one of his friends told her that likely wouldn't happen. According to him, her dad would probably stay in hiding forever.

Pushing past the loss of her parents, she continued to piece herself back together. The demons climbed on her back as they had David's, trying to keep her from doing what she knew to be right, but she persevered as she knew David had. Slowly but surely she began to build a life for herself in Hawaii and in the Church.

Then she met Trevor, a returned missionary who grew up in California and served his mission in Hawaii. He loved the area so much he came back to go to school. That's where Alice met him. She had started taking some classes herself at Brigham Young University, Hawaii. Studying music, she said. Piano pedagogy. Trevor overheard her practicing one day and asked her to go to dinner with him because of it. Six months later they were engaged, with plans to build their new lives together staying in their island paradise.

✦ ✦ ✦

Three months after the surprise visit, David and Jeanie stood in a line in Hawaii, shaking hands at the wedding reception. The wedding itself had been beautiful. Alice simply glowed. Trevor looked like the happiest man on earth. David had no doubt that this young man and Alice would take good care of each other.

Here at the reception, David and Jeanie stood in place of Alice's parents in the line, though they didn't have to explain their relationship with her to anyone. Each and every person in attendance knew all about David and what he had done for Alice. Before long he began to feel a bit embarrassed by the praise. Whatever she told them about him, she had overdone it.

Nobody lavished their appreciation more fervently than Alice's Aunt Amelia, who also stood in the line. David enjoyed seeing Amelia again, though he might have wished she'd stop talking about him quite so often.

Still, none of the embarrassing attention mattered as he watched Alice and Trevor. They were the picture of happiness. A radiant couple. Alice had said during her visit a few months previous how she couldn't wait to start a new family. She still missed Lily, but now she knew that she would see her again some day. In the meantime, Alice had come to realize she had a whole life yet to live. She wanted to be a mother again soon, and Trevor was equally thrilled about becoming a father.

Observing the beaming form of Alice as she embraced each and every guest, joy seemingly reflecting off her person in a thousand different angles, David swallowed back emotion. He sent another prayer of gratitude skyward for the chance to be a part of something so joyous.

There were times in his own early life when he felt certain that God had turned a blind eye on him. But he knew now, and had known for many years, that had not been the case. Even during the times when he felt most alone, David realized in retrospect that God had stayed with him. God needed him to be strong. He had something special in mind for David. Someday he knew he would understand the full reasons of why he had to go through what he did, but he could catch glimpses already.

One obvious reason was so that he could talk to people who were empty of hope and full of despair, as Alice had once been. David could look these people in the eye, as he had done to others like her more times these past several years than he could count, and tell them things do get better. He could tell them with unwavering certainty that joy waits for them at the other end of the storm, and lots of it.

They need only hold on tight and reach out for the hand that is already there.

# David John Dickson

David John Dickson has been a writer at heart since childhood. His education was in technical writing, though his true love in writing has always been, and will ever be, storytelling, from stage and screenplays to novels. He and his wife, April, live in Arizona with their two children.

# David Briggs

David Briggs and his wife, Jeanie, have seven children and twenty grandchildren (and are still counting). For twenty-two years, David successfully ran a roofing business. He sold the roofing business several years ago and now owns and operates a state-of-the-art sheet metal manufacturing plant in southeast Idaho.

0  26575 79835  7